# Brownie Guide Badge Book

D1362860

**THE GUIDE ASSOCIATION**

Published by The Guide Association
17–19 Buckingham Palace Road
London SW1W 0PT
E-mail chq@guides.org.uk
Web site www.guides.org.uk

The Guide Association
incorporated by Royal Charter, registered charity number 306016

© The Guide Association 1995
This edition first published 1995
Reprinted 1996 (twice), 1998, 1999, 2000

ISBN 0 85260 130 1
The Guide Association Trading Service ordering code 64048

Edited by Kathryn Cleary
Designed by Gillian Webb
Illustrated by Jan Lewis

Origination by
Ebony

Printed and bound by
Jarrold Printing

Users are reminded that during the lifespan of this
publication there may be changes to
The Guide Association's policy or practice by governing bodies
that will affect the accuracy of the information
contained within these pages.

# Contents

# Introduction

Do you have a particular interest or hobby? Would you like to do a badge based on that hobby?

In this book you will find details of all the Brownie Interest Badges and Staged Badges. The range is very varied and you may choose to do as many or as few as you like. Talk to your Guider, parents or guardians and teachers or instructors to help you decide on your next badge. (Don't be tempted to work on more than one at a time.) For every badge you gain you will receive a cloth badge to sew on your badge sash and the signature of the tester under the appropriate syllabus.

Brownie Interest Badges are brown and triangular in shape. Staged Badges are green and square, one badge for each stage. For these, you do not have to start at Stage 1 and you do not have to work through each stage unless you want to do so. For instance, whilst you might be a school chess champion and so could start at Stage 2 or 3 of the Chess Badge, you may be a beginner at photography so that you would start at Stage 1 of that badge. You may then move on to the next stage of the badge or miss out a stage and take a higher stage later, perhaps as a Guide.

For some of the badges you are asked to write things down. You may use a word processor or typewriter rather than handwriting if you so wish. You may also communicate by using sign language, Braille, art or collage work. If you are not physically able to do a required clause in a badge, you can instruct another person instead. Alternatively, your Guider and the tester may adapt that particular clause to meet your needs or set another clause that is equally challenging.

Badges will be tested in your first language. You do not have to take the tests in English if this is not your native language, although you may wish to take them in English nevertheless. Remember, it is your choice.

At the beginning of some of the syllabuses you will find notes and/or hints. The notes refer to the syllabus and the hints point you in the direction of sources of information. If you need further explanation or help, talk to your Guider, teacher or instructor, or go to your local library.

Finally, don't forget that your *Brownie Guide Handbook* has spaces for you to fill in the badges you gain as you go through Brownies. In your Handbook you can read about how Jill prepared for her Artist Badge, whilst Linda first chose Swimmer.

Which badge will *you* choose?

# Agility

1  Show that you can stand, sit, walk, run, jump and land well.

2  Turning the rope backwards, skip for half a minute without a break. Skip three fancy steps.

3  Show that you can perform a leap-frog.

4  Balance walk along a narrow bench or on flower pots over a distance of 6 m.

5  Join *two* of these actions into a sequence:
   - a forward and backward roll
   - a shoulder stand
   - a handstand against a support.

6  Make three different movements on the floor. These should follow one another and you should go at different speeds and in different directions so that you can make a pleasing pattern for someone to watch.

## Brownies with Disabilities Only

**Note**
You may have help from a person or an aid where you need it.

1  Show that you can do *at least two* of the following well:
   - walk
   - sit
   - crawl
   - stand
   - move backwards and forwards.

2  Travel along a bench 2 m long.

1

3 Do *one* of the following:
- a forward roll
- a backward roll
- a sideways roll
- a shoulder stand
- a handstand
- a balance on a different part of your body from usual.

4 Do *two* of the following:
- From a distance of 4m throw a 17cm ball or football through a 70cm hoop.
- From a distance of 4m throw a tennis ball to hit a target approximately 30cm square and 1.5m from the ground.
- From a distance of 4m roll a ball between two skittles 15cm apart.
- Throw a ball 10m underarm or overarm and catch it when it is thrown back to you.
- Throw a bean bag from 2m away to land on a 1m square on the ground. The bean bag must land in the square four times out of six.

5 Cover a distance of 80m in *one* of the following ways:
- by running
- by walking
- by self-propelled wheelchair
- by swing-through (walking with two aids).

Make a note of the time it took you and try to improve on that time within one month.

6 Make three different movements on the floor. These should follow one another and you should go at different speeds and in different directions so that you can make a pleasing pattern for someone to watch.

Date .................................

Tester .................................

Comments ..........................

..........................................

..........................................

# Artist

1 Know the primary colours and how to mix them to make other colours.

2 Use three colours to make a pattern. The pattern need not be a repeating one and you can use any method you like to make it, for example, potato cuts, home-made stick prints or coloured paper. Suggest a suitable use for the pattern, such as a book cover or printed scarf.

3 From your own observation or imagination make a picture using paints, crayons, inks or other colouring materials.

4 Make *two* of the following:
   - an invitation for a Brownie event
   - an illustrated prayer card for use in the Pack
   - a book mark
   - a greetings card
   - a poster.

5 At the test, draw or paint a picture of a subject agreed upon in advance by you and the tester.

Date ....................................

Tester ..................................

Comments ...........................

....................................................

....................................................

3

BROWNIE GUIDES

# Athlete

1 When you decide with your Guider to start working for this badge, make a chart to reflect what you can already do. The chart should show:

a how high you can jump

b the number of times you can skip in good style

c how far away from a target 50cm in diameter you can stand and throw a ball to hit the target at least four times out of five.

During at least six weeks, practise regularly and record on the chart how much you have improved. This will show whether you are ready to be tested.

2 At the test you must also:

a run 80m in 19 seconds

b run, walk or jog (you can do some of each) 1,000m in 8 minutes.

Date...................................

Tester.................................

Comments...........................

..........................................

..........................................

**You should always practise the clauses with other people. Use a soft landing area when jumping and only go on the road if there is nowhere else.**

# Bellringer

## Church Bellringing

### Notes

• For all stages you should show that you attend practices and Service ringing regularly.

• It may be necessary to do some of the clauses at a tower other than your own.

### Stage 1

1   Ring rounds correctly, leading and following.

2   Lower a bell unaided.

3   Be able to follow simple call changes accurately and explain the difference between two named change patterns such as 'Queens', 'Tittums', 'Whittingtons' and 'Reverse Queens'.

4   Name the parts of a tower bell and explain the function of each. Explain how the revolution of the bell produces hand and back strokes.

5   Explain how bells are made and tuned.

6   Know the location of the six nearest peals of bells to your home tower, the number of bells in each and the weight of the Tenor. If possible, visit and ring rounds at two of these towers and tell the tester of your experiences.

### Stage 2

1   Raise a bell unaided.

2   Show that you can put a 'whipping' on a rope end.

3   Know the importance of rope maintenance and how to change a rope.

4   Read a book on the history of bells or bellringing.

5   Be able to tell the tester about your local ringing association, for example, its name, membership requirements, the name of the Ringing Master and the Secretary.

6   Visit and ring at six towers other than your own.

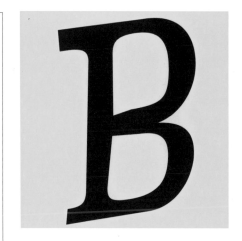

**B**

7 **Either**

For a Call Change Tower, ring an inside bell for the calling of a minimum of 60 changes.

or

For a Change Ringing Tower, ring an inside bell for the calling of a minimum of 60 changes.

or

For a Change Ringing Tower, ring the treble to a touch of Plain Minor and an 'inside' bell to a plain course of a Doubles method.

Show that you know what is meant by 'passing the treble' and explain how this is used to assist in the ringing of two methods.

## Stage 3

1 Ring up and down in peal.

2 Show that you can complete long and short splices.

3 Know about the history of the bells in your own tower and write an article about it for your church magazine or newsletter.

**Either**
For a Call Change Tower:

4 Conduct a touch.

5 Ring an inside bell to an acceptable competition standard. (The bells should start and finish in the down position and a minimum of 60 changes should be used.)

or

For a Change Ringing Tower:

4 Conduct 120 changes of Doubles from a bell affected at calls.

5 Ring a quarter peal.

6 Ring 720 changes of a Minor method inside.

## Stage 4

1 Demonstrate the ability to complete an eye splice.

2 Spend a total of three hours in direct contact with visitors or ringing learners at open events or ringing training sessions.

3 Write an article (such as might be published in your church magazine) for possible ringing recruits, explaining how they will be taught.

**Either**

For a Call Change Tower:

4 Conduct 'Sixty on Thirds' from memory.

5 Lead up *and* down in peal.

or

For a Change Ringing Tower:

4 Conduct 720 changes of Minor.

5 Lead up or down in peal.

6 Ring the plain course of a Surprise method on an inside bell and be able to write out one lead of a Surprise method which you have not rung, starting only with the place notation. Draw the line for a working bell and mark the place bells.

## Change Ringing on Handbells

### Stage 1

1 Name five parts of a handbell and describe how it is rung for change ringing.

2 Describe the system of numbering used in the set of bells which you ring.

3 Explain the technical terms used in ringing in your group.

4 Show that you understand the importance of care and maintenance of the metal and moving parts of a handbell.

5 With rhythmical precision, ring a pair of handbells correctly in rounds.

6 Show that you have attended a group on a regular basis.

### Stage 2

1 Name six parts of a handbell and describe how it is rung for change ringing.

2 Describe two systems of numbering used in handbell ringing.

3 Show that you know the importance of handbell care, maintenance and adjustment.

4 With rhythmical precision – using the hand stroke and back stroke positions – ring a pair of handbells correctly in rounds.

5 Show that you have attended a group on a regular basis.

### Stage 3

1 Be able to give a short talk on the history of the handbell to a Ranger Unit or similar group.

2 Explain the technical terms used in ringing in your group.

3 Ring a pair of handbells using two methods, including 'Bobs' and 'Singles', consisting of 120 changes on five bells and 720 changes on six bells.

4 Show that you have attended a group on a regular basis.

# Tune Ringing on Handbells or Chimes

## Stage 1

1 Name three parts of a handbell or chime and describe/demonstrate the method of ringing that your team usually uses for tune ringing.

2 Show that you understand the importance of the care and maintenance of the metal and moving parts of a handbell or chime.

3 Be able to read and explain simple music written in *one* of the following:
- staff notation
- tonic sol-fa notation
- alphabetical notation
- numerical notation.

4 Handling at least two handbells or chimes and reading from one of the notations listed above, play three tunes.

5 Show that you have attended a group on a regular basis for at least two months.

## Stage 2

1 Be able to complete all the requirements listed for Stage 1.

2 Either

Name six parts of a handbell and explain their functions.

or

Name the main parts of a handchime and explain their functions.

3 Handling at least two handbells or chimes and reading from one of the notations given in Stage 1 Clause 3, play a selection of four tunes to include:

a a tune involving half beats

b a tune involving a repeat, where you play a section again

c two tunes in simple harmony.

4 Take part in a public performance, playing at least three tunes.

5 Take part in the regular cleaning/maintenance routines used by your team.

6 Show that you have attended a group on a regular basis for at least three months.

## Stage 3

1 Be able to complete all the requirements listed for Stage 2.

2 Show that you know how to keep handbells or chimes in good working order, including simple 'first aid' measures of repair that can be safely used, storage, etc.

3 Handling at least two handbells or chimes and using one of the notations listed in Stage 1, Clause 3, ring a programme of tunes lasting at least ten minutes. The programme should demonstrate full use of changes in tempo (speed), dynamics (loud and soft playing) and ringing techniques, for example, shakes, damping, etc.

4 Either

Arrange a tune in simple harmony and teach it to your group.

**or**

Give a short talk on the history and development of handbells or chimes to a Ranger Unit or similar group.

5 Show that you have attended a group on a regular basis for at least six months.

**Stage 1**
Date.................................
Tester.................................

**Stage 2**
Date.................................
Tester.................................

**Stage 3**
Date.................................
Tester.................................

**Stage 4**
Date.................................
Tester.................................

# Bird Watcher

**Hint**

Information can be obtained from The Royal Society for the Protection of Birds, The Lodge, Sandy, Bedfordshire, SG19 2DL.

**Stage 1**

1 Keep a list of birds which can be seen around your home during one month.

2 Keep a notebook on at least three bird-watching expeditions and show this to the tester. The notebook should contain date, time, place, weather, which species of bird you saw, and what the birds were doing.

3 Talk to the tester about ways of watching birds without disturbing them.

4 Tell the tester how you can help birds in both summer and winter.

5 Find out if there is a club for young ornithologists in your area.

**Stage 2**

1 Show the tester the equipment you use for bird watching. Include clothing, and reference books and binoculars if you have them. Show that you can use binoculars correctly. ▶▶▶

**B**

2 Keep a notebook on at least ten bird-watching outings. Identify the birds you see, and observe and describe some bird behaviour. Talk about your observations with the tester.

3 Make a simple chart showing the birds which you see around your home. Mark on the chart the months when you see them.

4 Draw a rough outline of a bird and mark on it the following parts: crown, back, rump, belly, breast, primaries, flank.

5 Be prepared to identify the pictures of ten species of birds common to your area.

6 Tell the tester about some local places where you go to watch birds, which species visit these places and which nest there.

### Stage 3

1 Demonstrate the use and care of your bird-watching equipment. Tell the tester about the bird books you use and how and when you use them. Explain what is meant by the 'scientific order' which is used in most books.

2 Keep notes for at least six months on birds (and other wildlife) you see and interesting behaviour you observe. Use illustrations as well as written notes. Show the notebook to the tester and discuss entries.

3 Carry out a simple survey of birds visiting a particular study area: your parish, a local park, or some other place you visit regularly. (An area larger than a garden is necessary.) Your survey could be a series of counts, a census of birds during the breeding season, a line transect or some other generally accepted form of survey.

4 Draw the rough outline of a bird and mark on it the following parts: crown, rump, beak, belly, breast, primaries, flank, upper tail, coverts, tarsus speculum, supercilium, eye-stripe, nape, mantle, secondaries and wing coverts.

5 Demonstrate to the tester that you understand what is meant by migration. Explain the methods by which ornithologists have found out about birds' migration journeys.

Name five summer migrants and five winter migrants which you could reasonably expect to see in your local area.

6 Describe some British habitats and explain the threats to them. Which species of bird are endangered by these changes?

7 Describe how a nature reserve can be managed (looked after and developed) to make it more suitable for birds. Tell the tester about any reserves that you have visited and your impressions of them.

## Stage 4

1 Show the tester your bird-watching equipment, clothing and the books you find most useful. Discuss why and when you use particular books. Explain the order in which species are generally placed. Also, discuss the merits (or otherwise) of optical equipment. Explain the magnification of binoculars and the occasions when a telescope can be useful.

2 Show the tester your notebook(s) covering a full year's bird watching. Illustrations and written notes about numbers and behaviour should all be included. Discuss the excursions with the tester.

3 Be prepared to identify by sight 20 or more species, most of which are found in the United Kingdom, but also a few others which are only rare visitors or more commonly found in mainland Europe. Say which are resident, summer migrants, passage migrants, etc. Also, be prepared to identify or to be asked to describe the songs and calls of not more than ten common species.

4 Carry out voluntary work on a bird reserve or nature reserve. Discuss with your tester the importance of the reserve for wildlife and give an account of your activities.

5 Choose five species of bird which are threatened in the United Kingdom. Discuss the threats and the possible solutions with the tester.

6 Discuss with the tester the various types of census and survey that amateurs can help with.

7 Use your knowledge of, and interest in, ornithology to help another person prepare for Stage 1 or Stage 2.

| Stage 1 | |
| --- | --- |
| Date ................................. | |
| Tester ................................. | |
| **Stage 2** | |
| Date ................................. | |
| Tester ................................. | |
| **Stage 3** | |
| Date ................................. | |
| Tester ................................. | |
| **Stage 4** | |
| Date ................................. | |
| Tester ................................. | |

B

**B**

BROWNIE GUIDES

# Booklover

1   Make a list of six or more books you have enjoyed reading. Talk to the tester about them.

2   With the help of the tester choose four other books to read. When you have finished them, talk to the tester about them.

3   Show that you know how to cover a new book to keep it clean. Make a book mark.

4   Show how to use a simple reference book and an index.

Date.....................................

Tester...................................

Comments............................

...........................................

...........................................

12

# Canoeist

**Where there is reason to believe that the level of water pollution or low temperatures may render capsize drill potentially hazardous, alternative safer locations, including swimming pools, may be used for those clauses marked with an asterisk (∗).**

### Note
Throughout this syllabus the abbreviation BCU is used for the British Canoe Union.

### Stage 1

**Notes**

• The test may be taken in a canoe or kayak with an open or closed cockpit on still water. A spray-deck need not be worn.

• If you hold the BCU 1 Star or BCU Grade 1 Placid Water Test and complete Clause 1, you may have this badge.

• The tester for Clauses 2 to 8 should hold BCU Supervisor (Leader), Placid Water Teacher, Instructor or a higher qualification, or be a person with experience or a qualification approved by the County Assistant Outdoor Activities Adviser (Boating). The tester should look for performance at the standard expected for BCU 1 Star or Placid Water Tests Grade 1.

1  Swim 50 m and stay afloat for five minutes wearing clothes. (This clause may be done in a swimming pool and you may wear a buoyancy aid if you wish.)

2  Wear suitable clothing and a buoyancy aid for the test and be able to explain their importance to the tester. Know how to check your boat is safe before going afloat.

3  Launch the canoe and get into it.

4  Demonstrate alone or with a partner of similar ability:

   **a**  forward paddling over a distance of at least 100 m

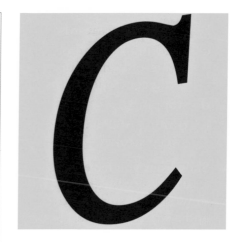

**b** paddling backwards

**c** paddling a circuit or figure-of-eight course using controlled turns

**d** stopping

**e** turning 360° using sweep strokes.

5 Show that you have made a satisfactory beginning in draw stroke, stern rudder and a support stroke.

6 Return to the edge and get out.

7 Know what to do if you capsize. If using a closed-cockpit kayak, demonstrate how to capsize and swim ashore.*

8 Know the Canoeist's Code of Conduct.

9 Hold a small first aid kit and know how to use it correctly.

## Stage 2

### Notes

• If you hold the BCU2 Star, the BCU Grade 2 or 3 Placid Water Test, or BCU Grade 2 Surf Test and complete Clauses 1 and 9, you may have this badge.

• The tester for Clauses 2 to 9 should be qualified as BCU Instructor or Placid Water Instructor, or hold a higher BCU qualification or a qualification approved by the County Assistant Outdoor Activities Adviser (Boating). This person may also test Clause 1. The tester should look for performance at the standard expected for BCU 2 Star or Grades 2 or 3 Placid Water Tests.

1 Swim 50m and stay afloat for five minutes wearing clothes. This clause may be done in a swimming pool and you may wear a buoyancy aid if you wish.

2 Show the tester your clothing and equipment and discuss why it is safe and suitable. Show some knowledge of the clothing and buoyancy aids for different conditions and of the materials used for boats and paddles.

3 Launch and get into your canoe. Fit a spray-deck if appropriate.

4 Demonstrate alone or with a partner of similar ability:

**a** efficient forward paddling over at least 200m

b paddling backwards (keeping the boat straight while showing good paddling style)

c the skills needed to paddle a figure-of-eight course – doubles

partners must paddle both back and front

d draw strokes on both sides keeping the boat in a straight line

e support strokes on both sides whilst stationary and on the move – in a kayak show high and low brace

f stern rudder

g 'J' stroke, if tested in an open canoe.

5 Show a satisfactory beginning in *two* of the following:

- sculling draw and sculling for support in a kayak
- sculling and cross-deck sculling in an open canoe
- eskimo rescue*
- ferry glide
- breaking into and out of moving water
- bow cut (bow rudder).

6 Go ashore showing correct approach relative to wind and current and get out.

7 Know what to do if you capsize and

**Either**
If using a kayak, demonstrate capsize with spray-deck fitted, being rescued and getting back into your boat in deep water, and rescuing another paddler in deep water.*

**C**

or

If using an open canoe, jump out and climb back in unaided.*

8  Know the Canoeist's Code of Conduct. Answer questions about safety and access in the area where you paddle (for example, dangers of weirs, currents, tides, group control and signs, the effect of weather, launching sites, access agreements, etc.).

9  Know how to recognise and deal with hypothermia. Describe to the tester the injuries that might happen when canoeing and what you would do.

## Stage 3

### Notes

• If you hold the BCU 3 Star, Inland Proficiency, Sea Proficiency, or both Grades 2 and 3 of Placid Water Tests and complete Clause 1, you may have this badge.

• The tester for Clauses 2 to 8 should be qualified as BCU Senior Instructor or hold a qualification approved by the County Assistant Outdoor Activities Adviser (Boating).

1  Swim 50m and stay afloat for five minutes wearing clothes. This clause may be done in a swimming pool and you may wear a buoyancy aid if you wish.

2  Present yourself for the test suitably dressed and equipped. Be prepared to explain your choice of gear to the tester.

3  Launch your boat and get in. Return to shore and get out.

4  Paddling alone, demonstrate that you are proficient at moving and controlling the canoe using all the following strokes appropriate to your boat — forward paddling, reverse paddling, sweep strokes, draw strokes, stern rudder, recovery strokes, sculling draw, sculling for support, bow rudder/bow cut, cross-bow cut, bow draw (open canoe), emergency stop, backwater stroke/cross-deck backwater stroke, 'J' stroke.

5  Capsize, swim ashore and empty your canoe with assistance if required.*

6  Capsize in deep water and be rescued by another paddler.*

7  Rescue another paddler from deep water. (Another person may be asked to help you but you must remain in charge of the rescue.)*

8  Answer questions to show that you know about:

a  the Canoeist's Code of Conduct

b  types of canoe and paddle

c  the river grading system and access to local waters

d  how to paddle in a group

e  the use of tow lines

f  the hazards that may be encountered on open water, rivers and sea

g  specific local features

h  the general effect of tide, wind and current

i  where to obtain weather forecasts and information.

16

9 Know how to recognise and deal with hypothermia. Demonstrate what you would do:

a to stop bleeding

b to identify and treat a broken bone

c to treat an unconscious breathing patient.

Using a manikin, show how to give expired air resuscitation.

**Stage 1**
Date.................................

Tester.................................

**Stage 2**
Date.................................

Tester.................................

**Stage 3**
Date.................................

Tester.................................

# Chess

## Stage 1

**Note**

If you hold the Preliminary Certificate of Merit of the British Chess Federation and complete Clause 5, you may have this badge.

1 Set out a chess board, ready for a game to be played.

2 Demonstrate the moves that each piece can make.

3 Know the rules of the game.

4 Understand the meaning of check and checkmate.

5 Observed by the tester, play a game with another player of a similar standard.

►►►

*C*

## Stage 2

**Note**

If you hold the Intermediate Certificate of Merit of the British Chess Federation and complete Clause 4, you may have this badge.

1 Complete Clauses 1 to 4 of Stage 1.

2 Be able to use the algebraic system of chess notation recognised by the World Chess Federation.

3 Demonstrate the use of:
   a castling
   b taking procedure with pawns.

4 Observed by the tester, play a game with another player of a similar standard.

## Stage 3

**Note**

If you hold the Higher Certificate of Merit of the British Chess Federation and complete Clause 5, you may have this badge.

1 Complete Clauses 1 to 3 of Stage 2.

2 Understand and demonstrate the following basic patterns:
   a the knight fork
   b the pin
   c the skewer.

3 Show checkmate positions on a chess board using:
   a rooks
   b bishops.

4 Demonstrate two openings to the tester.

5 Observed by the tester, play a game with another player of a similar standard.

## Stage 4

**Note**

If you hold the Advanced Certificate of Merit of the British Chess Federation and complete Clause 5, you may have this badge.

1 Complete Stage 3.

2 Demonstrate the following moves:
   a king's gambit
   b queen's gambit
   c 'greek gift' checkmate attack from a position set up by the tester.

3 Be able to recognise a range of strategies that

can be used in a game, and describe the moves which a player may make in order to win a game from three set end-game positions.

4 Analyse and comment on a written game set by the tester.

5 Observed by the tester, play a game against a player of your own standard or a higher one. (A time limit should be set by the tester.)

**Stage 1**

Date.....................................

Tester.................................

**Stage 2**

Date.....................................

Tester.................................

**Stage 3**

Date.....................................

Tester.................................

**Stage 4**

Date.....................................

Tester.................................

BROWNIE GUIDES

## Collector

1 Make an interesting, well-assorted collection to do with your hobby or interest. Your collection might be of picture postcards, soft toys, badges, novelty erasers or something else. Arrange and, if necessary, label your exhibits. The tester will judge your collection on the number of exhibits and their variety and arrangement.

2 Be able to tell the tester something about your collection, for example, how long you have had it, where the items came from, what you like about it, how you are going to extend it.

3 While you are working for this badge, go and see other collections, for example, in a library, an art gallery, a museum, a stately home, a garden or a zoo. Tell the tester about your visit and describe how the exhibits were displayed.

Date.....................................

Tester.................................

Comments...........................

.............................................

.............................................

# Communications

Choose *three* of the following:

1 Act or mime a scene from a recent Brownie event you have attended.

2 Out of talking range, send and read three short messages in semaphore or Morse.

3 Make a tape-recording of the sounds of five different animals.

4 Write or dictate a letter, poem or prayer and read it to the tester.

5 Look at magazines that you might buy. Tell the tester how they are the same, how they are different and which you prefer.

6 Show that you can set and record on video your favourite television programme.

7 Show how you are able to use Ceefax or Teletext to find out:

a news headlines

b the weather forecast

c television programme times.

8 Make a short recording of a story or magazine article you would like to share with a blind person of your own age.

9 Learn the manual (finger) alphabet and be able to:

a tell the tester your name

b ask the tester her/his name and understand her/his reply.

Date ................................
Tester ...............................
Comments ..........................
.........................................
.........................................

# Computer

## Stage 1

1 Tell the tester about the computer(s)/ printers, etc. with which you are familiar and explain the use of each item.

2 **Either**
Switch on a single computer, then load and run a program.

or

Use a computer connected to a network to log-on, select a program and run it.

3 Show how to type both small and capital letters and know the positions of the space, enter (return), delete and function keys.

4 Describe three uses of a computer in shops, factories, etc.

5 Keep a diary recording every time you use a computer for at least three months and take it with you to the test.

6 Learn how to play two new computer games, then explain to the tester how they are played, which you preferred and why.

## Stage 2

1 Complete Clauses 1 to 3 of Stage 1.

2 Describe to the tester a task which can be done both manually and using a computer, and explain the advantages and disadvantages of each method.

3 Choose *two* of the following and carry them out, using a computer, at the test:

- Use a word-processing package to produce a report of a Guiding event.
- Add, delete, amend and print records of a database.
- Use LOGO or a similar package to control a robot, turtle, etc. and make it follow a predetermined route.
- Use a graphics package to create a poster to publicise a Guiding event.
- Perform any other task of a similar level of difficulty.

## Stage 3

1 Complete Clauses 1 to 3 of Stage 1.

2 Describe to the tester one use of computers and their economic, legal and

moral effects on employees, employers and society.

3 Choose *three* of the following and carry them out accurately, using a computer, at the test:

- Use a word-processing package to produce a multi-page report of a Guiding event which includes double-line spacing, underlining, centring, etc.

- Use a desktop publishing package to produce a leaflet which promotes Guiding.

- Create a database to hold information about members of your Unit (for example, name, current Journey or Trefoil Badge worn, Interest Badge held, etc.) and be able to amend, interrogate and print records. Please be aware of the problems re the Data Protection Act in creating a database with 'live' data, that is data on actual members of the Unit.

- Use a spreadsheet package to create next year's income and expenditure budgets for the Unit and investigate what happens if subs are increased.

- Use a graphics package to create a poster to recruit either girls or leaders into Guiding.

- Perform any other task of a similar level of difficulty.

Stage 1

Date..................................

Tester..................................

Stage 2

Date..................................

Tester..................................

Stage 3

Date..................................

Tester..................................

BROWNIE GUIDES

# Conservation

1 Show the tester three examples of how you have practised conservation in your own home, for example, you may have made something useful out of second-hand or waste materials.

2 Tell the tester of three ways in which you might help with conservation inside your home and three ways out-of-doors.

3 Do *one* of the following clauses for eight weeks or more:

- Watch a small area of rough ground or a hedgerow. Keep a record (which you should update at least three times a week) of the different birds and insects you see in the area. Try to discover their feeding habits.

- Set up and maintain a bird table or feeding

place. Keep a record, not necessarily a written one, of all the visitors to this place.

- Help to plan and carry out an anti-litter campaign.

- Keep an illustrated record of visitors to a buddleia bush or other plant which attracts wildlife.

- Collect seeds of native trees. Successfully germinate two species and grow these until the first true leaves appear. Show these saplings to the tester and tell her/him what can be done with them.

- Find out about a world conservation project and make a poster to help promote it.

Date.....................................

Tester...............................

Comments..........................

.............................................

.............................................

*C*

# Cooks

## Stage 1

1 At the test make a snack, for example, egg on toast or a sandwich. Show skills that include the correct and safe use of equipment, such as a chopping board, knives, etc.

2 Show your skill at preparing fresh fruit and vegetables.

3 Show your skill at preparing a healthy dish that requires little or no heat, for example, fruit salad or salad.

4 Tell the tester what you understand by the term 'safety in the kitchen'.

5 Know how to wash up and clear away afterwards.

## Stage 2

1 Prepare a series of dishes showing culinary skills.

Your choice should take into account your culture and should include *two* items from each of the following groups:

- milk, cheese, yoghurt, soya milk
- fresh fruit and vegetables
- breads, cereals, rice, oats or pasta
- egg, fish, cheese, meat, poultry, tofu, peas, beans or other pulses.

2 Make a recipe book of the recipes you have tried and indicate whether they are tasty.

3 At the test, make a meal for yourself and the tester using convenience foods.

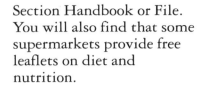

## Stage 3

1 Plan, cook and serve a two-course meal showing your competence in the following areas:

   a  method of cooking

   b  skills and safety in using a cooker/microwave

   c  presentation, including garnishing, serving and correct table laying.

2 Understand what is meant by a healthy diet and plan a week's menu accordingly. For advice, refer to your Section Handbook or File. You will also find that some supermarkets provide free leaflets on diet and nutrition.

3 Show your knowledge of good food hygiene practice when handling food, considering purchase, preparation and storage of food, and appropriate dress.

4 Using convenience foods create your own healthy dish at the test. Say which type of consumer would eat convenience foods.

## Stage 4

1 Over a period of six months, keep a record of recipes you make at home, school or college. Show you have improved your skills and how you can adapt recipes to suit dietary needs. Dishes chosen should be recipes new to you, from magazines and other such resources. Record your results — comments on how successful the dishes were and if they could be improved in any way. Comments could be from those who have eaten them.

2 Plan, cook and serve a meal for a group of people. Take a copy of the menu to the test and include planning and costings.

3 Take your favourite recipe to the test and show the tester how to make it. Explain why you have chosen it and describe its nutritional value.

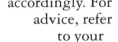

| Stage 1 |
| --- |
| Date................................. |
| Tester................................ |
| **Stage 2** |
| Date................................. |
| Tester................................ |
| **Stage 3** |
| Date................................. |
| Tester................................ |
| **Stage 4** |
| Date................................. |
| Tester................................ |

_C_

# Craft

Make _three_ of the following things. Finish two of them and take them to the test. Be ready to tell the tester how you made them and what you are going to do with them. Take the third, unfinished, thing to the test, so you can show the tester how you are going to finish it.

These are the things you can make:

- a collage using a variety of materials such as cloth, felt, wool and things from the natural world

- a model of anything you like, using suitable materials, for example, card, papier mâché or clay

- an article using material you have decorated by tie-dyeing, embroidery, vegetables printing, stencilling or some other method

- something useful that is woven

- an ornament made from a natural object such as a piece of wood or a stone that has an interesting shape. Clean it, rub it down and varnish it. Mount your object to make an ornament

- a simple flower arrangement to suit the time of year. Tell the tester how to make flowers and leaves last longer once they have been picked

- something else using another craft.

Date ...................................

Tester ...................................

Comments ...................................

...................................

...................................

# Crime Prevention

1 Tell the tester:

   **a** what you must tell your parents if you are going out without them

   **b** what you must remember to do if a stranger starts to talk to you.

2 Draw a picture and write a slogan which will encourage children to respect the property of other people and discourage vandalism.

3 Explain the property-marking schemes which use the postcode.

4 Do the following:

   **a** Get two leaflets about crime prevention from your local police. Explain their message to the tester.

   **b** Find out about the Neighbourhood Watch Scheme. What sign would tell you there is one in your area?

5 To protect your home from burglary explain what things should be checked:

   **a** if your family is going out

   **b** if your family is going on holiday.

Date ....................................

Tester ...............................

Comments .........................

............................................

............................................

27

# Culture

## Stage 1

1 Write down details of your own cultural background. These should include:

   a your nationality

   b the meaning of one of your names

   c your faith or religion

   d the flag of your country.

2 Visit a place of historical interest in the area in which you are living. If possible, make this visit with members of your Six, Patrol or Unit.

3 Know about a song, dance or craft which is from your own cultural background, or local to the area in which you are living.

4 Bring to the test a type of food which is traditional in your own culture or in the area in which you are living.

5 Talk to an adult known to you (other than a member of your own family) and from your own culture. Find out about their lifestyle.

## Stage 2

1 Find out where one or more of the adult members of your family group were born and talk to them about their lifestyle when they were your age. For example, you could ask the person what they wore for school, casual wear and special occasions, and about their home life, mealtimes, cooking, washing, hobbies, customs and festivals.

2 Know your own National Anthem and be able to sing it in your first language.

3 Find out about a well-known person connected with the locality in which you are living, and find a book in your local library which refers to her or him.

4 Learn a song, dance or craft from your own cultural background or local to the community in which you are living.

5 Cook a dish which is traditional in your own culture or in the area in which you are living.

6 Talk to an adult known to you (other than a member of your own family group) and from your own culture about her or his faith. Find out what they believe and why.

## Stage 3

1 Begin a record of your own family group.

2 Show in an interesting way (for example, using photographs, a scrapbook, a box of treasures or artefacts) the things which you think are important and show your cultural background. Before the test show this to your Six, Patrol or Unit.

3 Find out about the origin of the name of the village, district or town in which you are living. Discover how and why it developed as it did.

4 Teach your Six, Patrol or Unit a dance or craft from

your own culture or locality, and tell them about its origin or meaning.

5 Cook a simple two-course meal using traditional food and/or recipes from your own culture or from the area in which you are living.

6 Talk to someone from a different cultural background and find out about their lifestyle.

## Stage 4

1 Make a record of your family group, going back as far as possible.

2 Make a book to give as a gift to an overseas friend.

This should show as much as possible about you and your lifestyle, your local community and your country. This could be taken by you on a visit abroad, or given to someone to take back to their country, so watch the size and weight!

3 Tell a story or legend about your local community.

4 Make a leaflet or chart from which others could learn a dance or craft from your culture or locality.

5 Cook a simple two-course meal using food which is traditional to a culture different from your own and from the area in which you are living. Try to eat the meal in a traditional way (for example, for a Chinese or Japanese meal, use chopsticks and sit or kneel in the traditional manner).

6 Talk to someone from a different faith and cultural background and find out what she or he believes and why.

| Stage 1 |
| --- |
| Date................................. |
| Tester............................... |
| **Stage 2** |
| Date................................. |
| Tester............................... |
| **Stage 3** |
| Date................................. |
| Tester............................... |
| **Stage 4** |
| Date................................. |
| Tester............................... |

# Cyclist

**The Royal Society for the Prevention of Accidents recommends that all cyclists should wear safety helmets.**

**Hint**

For a copy of the Code of Practice on Safe Cycling, please send a stamped addressed envelope to Youth Activities, The Guide Association, 17–19 Buckingham Palace Road, London SW1W 0PT.

## Stage 1

1 Own or part-own a bicycle of the right size.

2 Keep your bicycle clean and know how to check it is in safe working order (if necessary, with adult help).

3 Know how to find out about lighting-up time. Know why lights and bright clothing are necessary when you are cycling.

4 Go with the tester for a ride showing that you can ride your bicycle safely (off-road), that you use the brakes correctly and that you understand:

   a the rules of the road for cyclists

   b the signals that cyclists give and observe

   c the correct way to turn right into a side road.

## Stage 2

1 a **Either**

   Attend a training course and pass the National Cycling Proficiency Test or equivalent test run by your local authority.

   or

   Ride your bicycle on a short route (on quiet roads) planned by the tester. Show that you can control your machine safely and confidently and be in the correct position on the highway. You must show you can start and stop safely. You will be asked to carry out left and right turns and an emergency stop. You should also know how cyclists use traffic lights, pedestrian crossings of all types, roundabouts and signed cycle routes in towns. Know how to park your bicycle safely.

   b Demonstrate cycle control in a safe area (such as a playground) by riding in and out of a line of blocks or, preferably, cones.

2 **a** Demonstrate how to check your bicycle is safe to use on the road (especially brakes, tyres and chain). Know how to maintain your bicycle in good working order.

**b** Know how to adjust the saddle and handlebars to a height correct for your use.

3 Have a practical knowledge of the Highway Code as it relates to you as a cyclist and tell the tester about the dangers of dark or loose clothing, personal stereos, badly arranged loads, carrying passengers, and inadequate lighting when cycling at night or in poor visibility.

4 Bring to the test records of at least three cycle rides to places of interest, one of which will have been of at least 10km (6 miles). If the routes include sections 'off-road', know the Off-road Cycling Code.

5 Make up a small first aid kit suitable for carrying on a cycle trip. Collect items for a simple tool and puncture repair kit. Bring both to the test and show a knowledge of their use.

## Stage 3

1 Clauses 1, 2 and 5 of Stage 2 must be passed.

2 Be able to read an Ordnance Survey map of suitable scale for cycling. At the test, plan a route between places suggested by the tester, taking into account traffic, terrain, etc. This can include 'off-road' sections if appropriate.

▶▶▶

3 Keep a record of three rides to places of interest, one to be of at least 24km (15 miles). The record should include details of prior planning, route taken and equipment carried. If routes are off-road, the Off-road Cycling Code must be observed.

4 Demonstrate at the test that you have a knowledge of suitable clothing for a cycle trip, taking into account your visibility to other road users, your personal safety and the weather conditions which may be encountered.

## Stage 4

1 Pass Clause 1 of Stage 3.

2 Plan and lead two cycling tours of at least 48km (30 miles) for three or four cyclists, on- or off-road. Keep a logbook of the tours.

3 Discuss your plans with the tester beforehand. The tester will wish to be satisfied that your map-reading, first aid and safety knowledge are adequate. (The permission of your parents or guardians must be obtained.)

4 Know the Off-road Cycling Code.

| Stage 1 |
| Date ................................. |
| Tester ................................ |
| Stage 2 |
| Date ................................. |
| Tester ................................ |
| Stage 3 |
| Date ................................. |
| Tester ................................ |
| Stage 4 |
| Date ................................. |
| Tester ................................ |

# Dancer

1 Do *one* of the following sections:

## Folk and National

Know three dances and be able to perform them really well.

## Modern Educational Dance

a Use *one* of these ideas to make up a simple dance:

- create a character
- make a pattern
- interpret a picture.

You can dance with or without sound.

b Perform a simple dance to:

**Either**

A rhythm played on a percussion instrument.

**or**

A piece of music which you have brought with you. You must be able to talk with the tester about the dance. She will be looking to see that you understand the use of your body.

## Ballet

You should hold the Lower Grade I Certificate of a school of dancing recognised by the Council for Dance Education and Training or any other recognised

▶▶▶

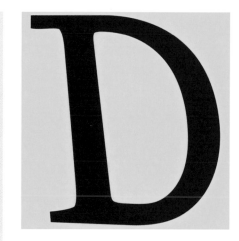

# D

equivalent certificate. At the test you will be asked to perform a dance lasting one minute using the steps in that grade.

## Ballroom

Choose and perform three ballroom dances. In each dance show that you can do at least three different steps.

## Wheelchair Dancing

Perform three dances of differing character in a self-propelled or assisted wheelchair.

### Other Forms of Dance

Hold the First Grade Certificate or Bronze Medal of any nationally recognised dance organisation in any other dance form.

2  Do *one* of the following:

- Make a scrapbook showing as many different kinds of dance as possible.

- Know the story of three well-known ballets.

- Choose three countries. Find out about their type of national dancing, the costumes worn and the sort of music used for accompaniment.

Date.................................

Tester...............................

Comments.........................

.........................................

.........................................

# Deaf Awareness

**Hint**

For further information contact the Royal National Institute for Deaf People (RNID). Look in the telephone book for the address of your nearest branch. The Head Office is at 105 Gower Street, London WC1E 6AH.

## Stage 1

1   Learn the manual alphabet and use it to:
    a   tell the tester your name
    b   ask the tester her/his name and understand her/his reply.

2   Find out and tell the tester about hearing dogs and their uses.

3   Take part in a game or activity with your Unit while wearing earplugs or headphones, making you unable to hear clearly.

4   Show the tester the correct way to approach a deaf person and how to speak to her or him in order for that person to lip-read.

## Stage 2

1   Using a sign language and, where necessary, the manual alphabet, show you can:
    a   introduce yourself to a deaf person and tell that person something about your home and a hobby you enjoy
    b   understand something the tester tells you about herself or himself.

Make sure you know how to say 'I don't understand'.

2   Know something about the work of one of the National Voluntary Organisations serving the needs of deaf people and those with a hearing loss, such as:
    •   Friends of the Young Deaf
    •   The National Deaf Children's Society
    •   Sense.

Share this information with members of your Unit.

3   Show the tester the symbol that indicates which facilities have provision for people with a hearing impairment.

4   Know the importance of facial expression and gesture when communicating with a deaf person. Find out what it is like to be deaf or to have a hearing loss by talking to someone with this disability, and tell the tester how it affects that person's life.

 D

## Stage 3

1 Be able to sign a simple story, poem or song and answer six questions signed to you, replying in sign language.

2 Find out something about a famous deaf person (for example, Jack Ashley MP, Evelyn Glennie, Elizabeth Quinn or Beethoven) and tell the tester what you have learned.

3 What hazards or difficulties could a deaf person encounter in daily living and what safety devices are available to help, for example, fire alarms, minicom, etc?

4 Take part in a social event with one or more members of the deaf community, for example, at a club, school or special unit, or by helping on a holiday or play scheme.

## Stage 4

1 Using sign language hold a conversation on a chosen subject with a deaf person for at least ten minutes.

2 Find out about the development of hearing aids to the present day, for example, the ear trumpet, phonic ear, etc. Give a talk about them to a group of people.

3 Investigate the difficulties faced by someone with a hearing impairment who has an additional disability, for example, blindness, and explain these difficulties to the tester.

4 Make up or adapt a game for a child with a hearing loss.

5 Complete *one* of the following:

- Design something which will enable a deaf person to become more independent.

- Show the tester how you would teach road safety to a child with a hearing loss.

- Show the tester how you would make a house safe for an elderly person with a hearing loss.

Stage 1
Date.................................
Tester.................................
Stage 2
Date.................................
Tester.................................
Stage 3
Date.................................
Tester.................................
Stage 4
Date.................................
Tester.................................

# Dinghy Sailor

**Note**

The following abbreviations are used throughout this syllabus:

- **IOCA** International Optimist Class Association
- **NSSA** National Schools Sailing Association
- **RYA** The Royal Yachting Association.

## Stage 1

**Notes**

• If you hold the RYA Young Sailors' Award Level 1, NSSA Bronze, IOCA Grade 1 or the RYA National Dinghy Certificate Level 1 and complete Clause 1, you may have this badge.

• The tester should be a qualified instructor or an experienced sailor over the age of 16 whom the County Assistant Outdoor Activities Adviser (Boating) considers suitable. Clauses 1 and 12 may be tested by this person.

1 Swim 50m and stay afloat for five minutes wearing clothes. This may be done in a swimming pool and you may wear a buoyancy aid if you wish.

2 Present yourself for the test in suitable clothing and put on a buoyancy aid correctly. Be able to explain why your clothing is suitable and why you wear a buoyancy aid.

3 Know the names of the basic parts of a boat: hull, mast, rudder, tiller, centreboard.

4 Be aware of wind direction.

5 Assist with rigging a dinghy.

6 Launch a dinghy and get underway with assistance.

7 Demonstrate that you can steer and turn a dinghy in light winds and when being towed.

8 Know, and if possible demonstrate, how to stay with your boat in the event of capsize.

9 Assist with coming ashore, recovery and putting away the dinghy and sails.

10 Know how to call for assistance and how to prepare to be towed.

11 Show that you can paddle or row a dinghy round a short triangular course.

12 Tie and know when to use a figure-of-eight (stopper) knot.

▶▶▶

## Stage 2

### Notes

• If you have the RYA Young Sailors' Scheme Stage 2, NSSA Silver, IOCA Grade 2 or the RYA National Dinghy Certificate Level 2 and complete Clause 1, you may have this badge.

• The tester for Clauses 2 to 10 should be an instructor or experienced sailor whom the County Assistant Outdoor Activities Adviser (Boating) considers suitable. This person may also test Clause 1.

1   Swim 50m and stay afloat for five minutes wearing clothes. This may be done in a swimming pool and you may wear a buoyancy aid if you wish.

2   Present yourself for the test in suitable clothing and a buoyancy aid. Be able to explain your choice of personal gear to the tester.

3   Know some ways of observing wind direction. Know what is meant by windward and leeward.

4   Rig a dinghy, with assistance if required.

5   Get underway from and return to a beach or pontoon in a light offshore wind.

6   Demonstrate in light winds under supervision:

   a   sailing a set course across the wind

   b   going about

   c   getting out 'of irons'

   d   stopping by lying wind abeam

   e   awareness of other water users and a basic understanding of the 'rules of the road'.

7   Crew a dinghy effectively showing adjustment of jib, centreboard and bodyweight.

8   **Either**
   Show how to capsize and right a single-handed dinghy.

   or

   Show how to be scooped in during recovery of a capsized dinghy.

9   Know how to prepare for a multiple tow.

10   Know how to tie and use a round turn and two half hitches, bowline and figure-of-eight (stopper) knot.

## Stage 3

### Notes

• If you hold the RYA Young Sailors' Certificate Stage 3 or the RYA National Dinghy Certificate Level 2 and complete Clauses 1 and 10, you may have this badge.

- The tester for Clauses 2 to 8 should be an RYA Instructor or hold a qualification approved by the County Assistant Outdoor Activities Adviser (Boating). This person may also test Clauses 1, 9 and 10.

1 Swim 50m and stay afloat for five minutes wearing clothes. This may be done in a swimming pool and you may wear a buoyancy aid if you wish.

2 Present yourself suitably dressed for the test and discuss your choice of clothing and buoyancy aid. Know how to check your boat is safe before going afloat.

3 Rig and launch a dinghy. Either demonstrate or show that you understand:

a how to launch in an onshore wind

b how to sail backwards from a pontoon in an offshore wind.

4 Understand how to adjust rigging to suit weather conditions. Reef a dinghy ashore.

5 Demonstrate that you can:

a tack proficiently

b gybe proficiently

c sail on a beat, reach and run

d apply the 'five essentials' (sail setting, balance, trim, centreboard and course made good)

e recover a 'man overboard'

f stop the boat

g return to shore, mooring or jetty safely.

6 Know the basic 'rules of the road' (port/starboard, windward boat and overtaking boat) and any particular conditions or hazards in the area in which you usually sail. Explain what precautions you would take before going afloat and where to obtain a weather forecast. ▶▶▶

**D**

**D**

7 Know what action to take when in distress and how to help others in distress.

8 **Either**
Show how to capsize and right a single-handed dinghy.

**or**

Show how to capsize a dinghy and be scooped in during recovery.

9 Tie and know when to use these knots: a figure-of-eight (stopper), round turn and two half hitches, bowline and reef.

10 Know how to recognise and deal with hypothermia. Describe to the tester how you would deal with cuts, a bang on the head, blisters and rope burn.

Demonstrate artificial respiration using a manikin.

## Stage 4
**Notes**
• If you hold the RYA Young Sailors' Scheme Advanced Sailing White Award or the RYA National Dinghy Scheme

Level 3 and complete Clause 1, you may have this badge.

• The tester for Clauses 2 to 15 should be an RYA Instructor or hold a qualification approved by the County Assistant Outdoor Activities Adviser (Boating). This person may also test Clauses 1 and 16.

1 Swim 50m and stay afloat for five minutes wearing clothes. This may be done in a swimming pool and you may wear a buoyancy aid if you wish.

2 Present yourself for the test wearing suitable clothing and a buoyancy aid. Be able to describe the standards used to grade buoyancy aids and what personal gear is suitable for different conditions.

3 Know what safety measures to take before going afloat and what equipment to take with you.

4 Rig and launch a dinghy to suit the weather conditions.

5 Leave and return to shore, jetty or mooring. Know, and if possible demonstrate, how to do this from both windward and leeward shores.

6 Sail to best advantage round a given course showing an understanding of balance, trim, centreboard, set of sails on different points of sailing, and course made good. Know and apply the basic 'rules of the road'.

7 Demonstrate that you can:

   a come alongside a moored boat

   b sail in close company with other boats

   c be towed

   d tow another sailing dinghy

   e heave-to

   f recover a 'man overboard'

   g reef afloat.

8 Know the principles of anchoring. Demonstrate that you can use and stow an anchor.

9 Know about buoyancy bags/tanks and how the distribution of buoyancy affects the capsized dinghy.

10 Demonstrate how to right a capsized dinghy, bail out and sail on.

11 Paddle and row a dinghy round a short triangular course.

12 Know the names for the parts of a boat and sails, and the terms for position relative to the boat and for boat manoeuvres.

13 Tie and know when to use these knots: figure-of-eight (stopper), round turn and two half hitches, sheetbend, clove hitch, rolling hitch, bowline and fisherman's bend. Demonstrate common whipping, heat sealing and eye splice.

14 Know why you need to be aware of the weather and how to obtain weather forecasts and information. Know the characteristics of high and low pressure areas, the significance of changes in barometric pressure and the Beaufort scale. Give a *simple* interpretation of a synoptic chart. ▶▶▶

**D**

**D**

15 Know the hazards and features of the waters you normally sail. If this is tidal water, be able to explain how to predict tides, the rule of twelfths, and the effect of wind, tide and current. Show that you can use the local tide tables.

16 Know how to recognise and deal with hypothermia.
Demonstrate:
a how to stop bleeding
b how to identify and treat a broken bone
c how to treat an unconscious breathing patient.

Using a manikin, demonstrate how to give expired air resuscitation.

| Stage 1 |
| Date................................... |
| Tester................................. |
| **Stage 2** |
| Date................................... |
| Tester................................. |
| **Stage 3** |
| Date................................... |
| Tester................................. |
| **Stage 4** |
| Date................................... |
| Tester................................. |

# Discoverer

1 Observe seven living creatures and seven living plants. Be able to name and discover something of interest about each of them.

2 Following directions you have been given, take your tester to a place unknown to you. This will not be more than 300 m away. To do this you may have to use a compass, follow signs on the ground or look for landmarks (which might be natural ones or buildings, etc.). The tester may ask you to do any one or more of these things.

3 During the test show that you know the Country Code, the Highway Code (as it applies to pedestrians) or the Blue Cross Code, whichever is most suitable to the area of your test.

Date ...............................

Tester ...............................

Comments ..........................

.........................................

.........................................

43

# Downhill Skier

**Hint**

For European alternative qualifications to those given in the syllabus, contact Youth Activities, The Guide Association, 17–19 Buckingham Palace Road, London SW1W 0PT.

## Stage 1

**Notes**

• Disabled skiers who cannot fulfil any of the requirements for Clauses 1 and 2 may demonstrate a controlled descent, turning and stopping, instead.

• This badge may be awarded if you hold the British Alpine Ski Award Two Star Award and pass Clauses 1b, 4c and 4d.

1   Demonstrate the following:

   a   carrying skis

   b   turning around in a limited space using a kick turn or step turn

   c   side-stepping up and turning on the slope

   d   a snowplough for controlled descent, at a slow speed, with ability to stop at any moment

   e   downhill traversing to the right and to the left

   f   getting up on a slope after a fall.

2   Make four linked snowplough turns.

3   Do a straight schuss without falling.

4   Understand:

   a   the principles of release bindings

   b   the adjustment of the bindings in use

   c   the principle of ski brakes and the reason why they are used

   d   the correct fit of a ski boot.

5   Show or describe suitable clothing and equipment for skiing on the following slopes:

   a   artificial

   b   snow in all weather conditions.

6   Know the safety rules that apply to skiing on either artificial slopes or snow slopes. Explain the procedure in the event of an accident.

## Stage 2

**Note**

This badge may be awarded if you hold the British Alpine Ski Award Three Star Award and pass Clauses 1d and 4.

1   Demonstrate the following:

   a   side-slipping (both sides)

   b   swinging to the hill from a steep traverse (both sides)

   c   rhythmically linked stem christies.

2   Make a controlled descent of at least 150m showing consideration to other skiers.

**D**

3  Make several successful ascents of either a ski tow (drag lift) or a chair-lift (using skis).

4  Know the symptoms of exposure and methods of treatment.

## Stage 3

### Note

This badge may be awarded if you hold the British Alpine Ski Award Four Star Award and pass Clause 1.

1  You must have skied on more than one slope.

2  Demonstrate at least ten long radius parallel turns with good leg extension.

3  Ski in control over bumps, absorbing them with your legs.

4  Make a controlled descent of a red run showing consideration for other skiers.

5  Choose the route on easier terrain, showing sensible choice of line and good awareness of hazards.

**Disabled skiers may use any necessary extra equipment, for example, outriggers.**

**D**

2 Choose a good route down a red run and ski down it without falling. Vary your techniques to suit the terrain.

3 Be able to demonstrate sound posture and the effective use of skis.

4 Know how to select, prepare and maintain skis.

5 Be able to find your way over a route using a resort map.

| Stage 1 | |
|---|---|
| Date.................................. | |
| Tester................................ | |
| **Stage 2** | |
| Date.................................. | |
| Tester................................ | |
| **Stage 3** | |
| Date.................................. | |
| Tester................................ | |
| **Stage 4** | |
| Date.................................. | |
| Tester................................ | |

6 Explain the dangers of a mountain environment.

### Stage 4

**Note**

This badge may be awarded if you hold the British Alpine Ski Award Five Star Award.

1 Demonstrate the following on snow:

a at least ten short swings, showing control of speed, rhythm and co-ordination

b at least ten parallel step turns

c at least ten parallel skate turns

d a terrain jump without a fall on landing.

# Faith Awareness

**Note**

• Each of the four staged badges should be taken with the support of a member of the worshipping community to which you belong or where you would like to start your quest for faith. Stage 1 is for you if you have no experience of a worshipping community. If you already attend classes organised by your place of worship, you will want to start on one of the later stages. Every clause is designed for you – you must fit it into your pattern of worship, your talents and abilities, and your interests. The adult helping you will want to be sure you have found out more about the faith of your choice than you knew when you started the badge, and that you have strengthened your understanding of the Promise. Don't forget to show this syllabus to her or him.

**Hint**

• If you wish to have a copy of this syllabus in another language or have any queries, please contact:
The Development Officer, Guiding Services, 17–19 Buckingham Palace Road, London SW1W 0PT.

## Stage 1

1  Attend your place of worship regularly.

2  Take part in an act of worship in your Unit.

3  Show members of your Unit an item or ritual used in your place of worship.

4  Draw or make a collage or a model of a religious celebration.

5  Talk to your Guider about a Good Turn you have done for your worshipping community and explain how it has helped you to understand your Promise.

## Stage 2

1  Attend your place of worship regularly. Draw a plan or  ▶▶▶

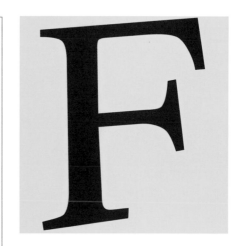

picture or take a photograph of your place of worship. Show this to a leader of your worshipping community and find out if she or he knows any interesting stories about it.

2 With your Six, Patrol or Unit, help to plan and carry out an act of worship in your Unit using mime, reading, music, dance, etc.

3 Read a book, watch a video or hear a story about someone whose faith plays an important part in her or his life. Talk to an adult leader about your chosen person, who may be someone in the past or present.

4 Find out about the meaning of a religious festival of your own faith. Tell your Six, Patrol or Unit what you have learned.

5 Find out about an organisation which is working for the good of others. Use your findings to help others understand the purpose of the organisation.

6 Choose or write a prayer which is about keeping the Promise and use it at a suitable occasion.

## Stage 3

1 Attend your place of worship regularly. Undertake a responsibility in some activity of your worshipping community.

2 Enable a group of young people to plan and carry out an act of worship.

3 Find six passages in your holy book which relate to current everyday situations. Explain (to an adult) why you chose them.

4 **Either**

Find out about the beliefs of at least two faiths or denominations different from your own.

or

Find out all you can about other opportunities for worship in your area.

5 Find out about the needs of a disadvantaged group in your local community. Find out how you and/or your Unit can be of service to them. Plan with others how to carry out this service.

6 Explain the meaning of the Promise to another member of The Guide Association. Choose or write a prayer within your faith which helps understanding of the Promise.

## Stage 4

1 Attend your place of worship regularly and undertake a responsibility within your worshipping community.

2 Oversee the planning of worship in your Unit for a term, ensuring that individual members and groups have the opportunity to plan and participate.

3 Study your holy book or sacred writings and be able to suggest suitable readings for two themes, such as peace, thanksgiving, forgiveness, our world, our community, etc. Find or compose prayers

5 Become involved with a project supported by your worshipping community.

6 Find a Promise that is different from each of the four World Regions. Discuss with your Commissioner the differences and what your own Promise means to you.

| | |
|---|---|
| **Stage 1** | |
| Date............................... | |
| Tester............................. | |
| **Stage 2** | |
| Date............................... | |
| Tester............................. | |
| **Stage 3** | |
| Date............................... | |
| Tester............................. | |
| **Stage 4** | |
| Date............................... | |
| Tester............................. | |

to fit the themes you choose and use them at a suitable occasion.

4 Know the places and patterns of worship in your area and be able to direct others to them.

# Fire Safety

**Note**

If you hold the Brownie First Aider badge, you are exempt from Clause 7.

1 Visit your local fire station or invite a fire officer to your meeting. Find out how the fire service works and what happens when a fire station receives an emergency call.

2 a Know how fires start and spread.

   b List ways in which fires can be prevented.

3 Be able to explain why smoke detectors should be used in homes and where they should be sited.

4 Tell the tester what you would do if a fire happened in your home. You must include:

   a warning and evacuating others

   b being able to prevent the spread of the fire

   c being able to call the fire service using the 999 system and passing on the important information.

5 a Know what to do if a person's clothes are on fire.

   b Show how you would crawl to safety from a smoke-filled room.

   c Know what to do with a chip-pan fire.

6 Know the importance of fire extinguishers. Be aware that different fire extinguishers are used on different types of fire.

7 Be able to deal with the following basic first aid situations:

   a unconsciousness

   b burns and scalds

   c shock.

Date.....................................

Tester...................................

Comments.............................

..............................................

..............................................

# First Aider

**Notes**

• Throughout the test you must show how you would reassure a patient and make her or him comfortable.

• If you hold *one* of the following certificates, you may have this badge:

  • British Red Cross Society, Junior First Aid Certificate

  • St John Ambulance Association, all three parts of the Three Cross Award

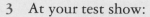

• St Andrew's Ambulance Association, Preliminary Certificate.

1 Understand the importance of getting adult help as quickly as possible in any accident. Know how to do this.

2 Show on a manikin that you can perform artificial ventilation by the mouth-to-mouth or mouth-to-nose method. Tell the tester of some accidents following which you might have to give artificial ventilation. Know what to do when the patient recovers.

3 At your test show:

  a how to control bleeding

  b how you would stop bleeding from the nose

  c how you would clean around and put a dressing on a grazed knee and cut finger.

4 Show how to treat burns and scalds.

5 a Show how you would deal with a minor graze.

  b Tell the tester how you would deal with a major graze and cut.

  c Know the importance of not removing a foreign body such as gravel, glass or splinters.

F

Date....................................

Tester..................................

Comments.............................

............................................

............................................

51

# F

# Friend
to Animals

**Note**

For the purpose of this badge, animal may mean amphibian, bird, fish, insect, mammal or reptile.

## Stage 1

1  With the owners' permission, get to know several different kinds of pet. Decide which would be right for you and which would be best for an old person living alone.

2  **Either**

   If an animal already lives in your house, explain to the tester how you attempt to care for it.

   **or**

   If you do not yet have a pet, check out your house to see if it is suitable. You need to think about:

   a  how much space your pet will need

   b  the amount of exercise it will require

   c  the type and cost of food it will eat

   d  how to keep it clean

   e  how much company it will need.

3  Find out about the best conditions for keeping *two* of the following animals happy and healthy:

   - cat
   - dog
   - rabbit or guinea pig
   - hamster, mouse or gerbil
   - goldfish, cold-water or tropical fish
   - stick insect
   - canary, budgerigar or parrot.

   You can make the information known to the tester in any way you choose.

## Stage 2

1  Take a full share in looking after your pet or another animal for at least three months. The other animal might belong to someone else, for example, you might help to look after an older person's dog, or it could be a classroom animal.

2  Arrange for the tester to meet your animal and tell her or him how you look

**For your safety, you should think carefully about the animal you choose and discuss the safety aspect with your Guider. This should be considered at each stage.**

after it. Do not forget to mention anything special it does.

3  Know what to do if you find a stray animal or lose your own animal.

4  Explain to the tester the differences between the work of the following:
a  PDSA or Blue Cross
b  RSPCA
c  a veterinary surgeon.

5  Know the obedience training for your pet where appropriate.

## Stage 3

1  For three months or more, look after an animal suitable for keeping as a pet.

2  Know the causes and treatment of two common diseases or two reasons why your animal could be unwell.

3  Visit an animal or bird sanctuary, refuge, reserve or somewhere similar. Describe to the tester what you learned there about the care of animals or birds.

4  Understand that close contact with some animals can pose health hazards for some people. Find out and discuss with the tester two possible health problems and how these could be avoided.

5  Pet owners have responsibilities. Discuss with the tester topics such as:
a  noise and nuisance
b  obedience training
c  local by-laws relating to animals.

## Stage 4

1  Take full responsibility (for at least three months) for an animal suitable for keeping as a pet.

2  Understand and be able to explain to a younger person how and why breeding is controlled in your selected animal.

3  Explore the possibilities of showing your selected animal. This should include the breed standards and any special requirements. Visit

a show and note what arrangements are made to prevent the animal suffering, for example, from heat or lack of water, during the show.

4  Using any interesting method, tell the story of St Francis, or an equivalent story in another religion, to a group of younger people.

5  Explain to a younger person why a working animal does not often make a suitable pet.

**F**

| Stage 1 | |
|---|---|
| Date | .................................. |
| Tester | .................................. |
| **Stage 2** | |
| Date | .................................. |
| Tester | .................................. |
| **Stage 3** | |
| Date | .................................. |
| Tester | .................................. |
| **Stage 4** | |
| Date | .................................. |
| Tester | .................................. |

# G

## Gardener

1 For at least four months cultivate and keep tidy a garden plot, window box or boxes, pots, etc. on greenhouse staging. Keep the tools you use in good condition.

2 Grow two kinds of vegetables and two kinds of annual flowers from seed. Tend and train them where necessary.

3 Transplant seedlings.

4 Gather some garden flowers and make an arrangement for someone else. You can use dried flowers if you wish.

5 Be able to recognise five garden weeds.

6 a Know the dangers of tools left lying around when working under wet and rainy conditions. The tools should include garden chemicals, electrical equipment, scissors, knives, pruning saws and hooks.

b Know how to deal with minor injuries, such as cuts, splinters and scratches.

Date....................................

Tester..................................

Comments............................

...........................................

...........................................

## Hobbies

1 Show a continuing interest in your chosen hobby for at least three months.

2 Demonstrate to the tester how you pursue your hobby and what equipment, materials and background information you have used.

3 Discuss with the tester how you plan to develop your hobby or skill in the future.

| Date............................... |
| Tester............................. |
| Comments...................... |
| ...................................... |
| ...................................... |

## Hostess

1 At your test you will be asked to:

a write a letter inviting a friend to tea, a party or to stay with you

b address the envelope correctly.

2 On your own, or with a friend, welcome and look after a guest or guests. This can be in your own home, at a party or at a Brownie event. Prepare the refreshments yourself, make a table decoration to put on the table or tray, and wash and clean up afterwards.

| Date............................... |
| Tester............................. |
| Comments...................... |
| ...................................... |
| ...................................... |

BROWNIE GUIDES

## House Orderly

**Note**

For this badge you should do all the clauses at your home and be ready to show or tell the tester what you have done or can do. She or he will ask you to do two of the clauses at the test.

1 Clean *two* of the following:
- a window
- a wash/hand-basin
- a cupboard
- brass or silver.

2 Tidy and dust your bedroom.

3 Hand wash a small item, for example, socks, necker, tea-towel or some other item.

4 Make your own bed every day for a week.

5 Lay the table for a midday or evening meal and wash up the dishes, cutlery and cooking utensils.

6 With adult supervision be able to do *two* of the following:
- use a vacuum cleaner
- clean a refrigerator (defrost if necessary)
- use a dishwasher
- use a food mixer
- use an electric kettle
- use a microwave oven
- use a washing machine
- use an iron.

If you choose either of the last two, you must also know the meaning of the symbols on the clothes' labels.

Date.....................................

Tester..................................

Comments...........................

..........................................

..........................................

# Interpreter

## Stage 1

**Note**

You should complete Clauses 1 and 2 and *two* others of your choice in one language other than your own.

1 **Famous people and places**

Find out about a famous place in a country where your chosen language is spoken.

2 **Using the language**

At the test, in your chosen language:

a tell the tester how you would order food and drink

b talk about your family.

3 **Phrases**

At the test, tell the tester how you would introduce yourself in your chosen language, for example, be able to say 'hello', your name and 'goodbye'.

4 **Exploration**

Visit or write to your nearest tourist office and find out how they could help somebody visiting the area for the first time.

5 **Creation**

Make a craft which is traditional from a country where your chosen language is spoken and know what it is called in that language.

## Stage 2

**Note**

You should complete Clauses 1 and 2 and *two* others of your choice in one language other than your own.

1 **Famous people and places**

Find out about a famous person from a country where your chosen language is spoken.

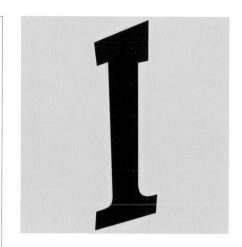

2 **Using the language**

At the test, in your chosen language, talk about:

a your life

b your hopes for the future.

3 **Phrases**

In your chosen language, help the tester to get around your city or town by teaching her or him useful phrases for shopping, travel (train or bus) and sightseeing.

4 **Exploration**

Find out about a country where your chosen language is spoken. Tell the tester about its capital, leader, location, currency (and its relative sterling value), weather and other issues.

5 **Creation**

Learn a song from a country where your language is spoken.

## Stage 3

**Note**

You should complete Clauses 1 and 2 and *two* others of your choice.

1 **Famous people and places**

Find out about a festival from a country where your chosen language is spoken.

2 **Using the language**

At the test, in your chosen language, talk about:

a your childhood

b your hobbies.

3 **Phrases**

In your chosen language, help the tester to get around your city or town by teaching her or him useful phrases for exchanging money and traveller's cheques.

4 **Exploration**

Find out about places where you can get help in an emergency in a country where your chosen language is spoken, for example, if you have lost your money, if someone needs to get home fast, or if someone is ill.

5 **Creation**

Cook some food from a country where your chosen language is spoken and know the names of the ingredients in that language.

## Stage 4

**Note**

You should complete Clauses 1 and 2 and *three* others of your choice.

1 **Famous people and places**

Find out about a current issue in a country where your chosen language is spoken.

2 **Using the language**

At the test, in your chosen language, talk about:

a an item of news

b Guiding in the United Kingdom.

3 **Phrases**

In your chosen language describe your favourite sport or talk about a hobby.

your chosen language is spoken.

6 **Guiding**

Take part in and use your language skills at an international Guiding event.

7 **Travel**

Travel in a country where your chosen language is spoken. Report back to the tester.

4 **Exploration**

Watch a TV programme or read an article about an issue currently affecting a country where your chosen language is spoken.

Talk to the tester about the issue and find out her or his perspective on it.

5 **Creation**

Cook or plan a meal where each course reflects the food eaten in a country where

| | |
|---|---|
| **Stage 1** | |
| Date | ................................... |
| Tester | ................................... |
| **Stage 2** | |
| Date | ................................... |
| Tester | ................................... |
| **Stage 3** | |
| Date | ................................... |
| Tester | ................................... |
| **Stage 4** | |
| Date | ................................... |
| Tester | ................................... |

# J

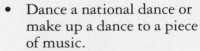

BROWNIE GUIDES

## Jester

Choose *three* of the following ways to entertain an audience:

- Recite a poem or tell a short story.
- Act, mime or use puppets to tell a story of an event from history.
- Dance a national dance or make up a dance to a piece of music.
- Sing with or without accompaniment.
- Play a piece on a musical instrument.
- Perform an item of your own choice. This could be juggling, conjuring or something else.

You can do this badge with a small group of other Brownies, but at least one of the three items must be performed on your own.

Date.................................

Tester...............................

Comments.........................

.........................................

.........................................

60

# Knitter

## Notes

• You can start at any stage but, if you start with Stages 2, 3 or 4, you must show that you can cast on and off.

• Knitting by hand or crochet is acceptable at any stage.

• Dolls' garments should not be included at any stage.

• Items used at one stage must not be presented again at any other stage.

## Stage 1

### Notes

• All items should be made out of school or college.

• If several girls are making squares, each must make at least three so that all the squares can be sewn together to make a rug or blanket for an old person or a charity. (See the craft publications listed in The Guide Association *Publications Catalogue* for ideas.)

1 At the test, show the tester that you can do the following:

**Either**
If you are knitting:

a cast on and off

b garter stitch (knit every row)

c stocking stitch (knit and purl rows alternately).

**or**

If you crochet:

a make a loop to start, then crochet a 20 cm chain and fasten off

b make at least four rows of double crochet on this chain base.

2 Use squares or diamonds (which should be at least 12 cm in size) to make two or more items that can be useful either in the home or to a person, for example, a dishcloth, mat, cushion, cot blanket, ball, purse or pot-holder. One of the items should show that you can change colours during the making. ▶▶▶

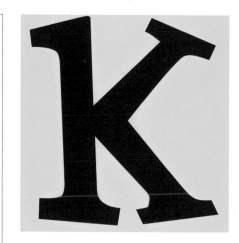

## Stage 2

**Note**

One item only may be made at school.

1. Choose a simple pattern and, following the instructions, make a garment for a child or baby using at least two different stitches, for example, single or double ribbing, garter, stocking or moss stitch. For crochet you may use a single, double or treble chain.

2. Make another item of your choice, for example, mittens with thumbs, a bobble hat, a scarf with tassel ends, a set of three fancy mats or a soft toy.

3. Know how to care for woollen items.

## Stage 3

**Note**

One item only may be made at school or college and one garment may be made with a knitting machine.

1. Following printed instructions, make a garment with sleeves, for example, a jumper or cardigan for a child, yourself or an adult. Know how to pick up a dropped stitch.

2. Show that you understand the following terms:

**Either**

If you are knitting:

a. pass the slip stitch over
b. wool forward
c. wool back
d. wool over needle
e. increase
f. decrease.

or

If you crochet:

a. double crochet
b. treble crochet
c. slip stitch
d. increase
e. decrease.

3. Demonstrating all the terms listed in the relevant section of Clause 2, as well as any other necessary stitches:

**Either**

Knit a pair of socks or gloves with fingers.

or

Crochet a garment or decorative item.

4. Make one other item of your choice.

5 All the items must be correctly finished and sewn up where necessary. At the test, you may be asked to demonstrate how this has been done.

6 Know how to launder and care for the items you have made. Be prepared to discuss with the tester the types of yarn used and the cost of each item.

## Stage 4

### Note

All items should be made out of school or college and one item may be made with a knitting machine.

1 Make a jumper, cardigan, waistcoat or sleeveless pullover for a child or adult using Fair Isle, Aran or another fancy pattern.

2 **Either**

Knit a small item to show the use of a cable needle.

or

Crochet a small item to illustrate the use of surface crochet or decorative edging.

3 Using leftover balls of wool, make a useful item(s) that can be given to a hospital, needy family or relief agency.

4 Discuss with the tester the different types of yarn used, their uses and costs.

**K**

| Stage 1 |
| --- |
| Date................................ |
| Tester................................ |
| **Stage 2** |
| Date................................ |
| Tester................................ |
| **Stage 3** |
| Date................................ |
| Tester................................ |
| **Stage 4** |
| Date................................ |
| Tester................................ |

# Knotter

**Hint**

If you can buy or borrow some of the following books you will find them useful:

• *Alternative Knot Book* by Dr Harry Asher, published by Nautical Books.

• *Knotting For Guides* by Hazel Bailey, published by The Guide Association.

• *The Knot Book* by Geoffrey Budworth, published by Paperfronts, Elliot Right Way Books, Kingswood, Surrey.

• *Knots, Ties and Splices* revised by Commander J. Irving, published by Routledge & Kegan Paul Ltd.

## Stage 1

1    Show that you can tie the following knots, bends and hitches:

    **a**  thumb knot

    **b**  double overhand knot

    **c**  reef knot

    **d**  surgeon's reef

    **e**  reef bow

    **f**  lark's head

    **g**  pedigree cow hitch

    **h**  round turn and two half hitches.

2    Choose from the knots, bends and hitches in Clause 1, and show that you can do the following:

    **a**  make hand loops at each end of a skipping rope

    **b**  tie a bow in shoe laces

    **c**  put a stopper knot at the end of a sewing thread

    **d**  fasten off a bandage sling

    **e**  put up a washing line with a different hitch at either end.

3    Make a single plait in a length of thin rope or cord.

## Stage 2

**Hint**

You should choose a suitable weight of string, cord or rope for each knot, bend or hitch.

1    Show that you can tie the following:

    **a**  figure-of-eight knot

    **b**  packer's knot

    **c**  fisherman's knot

    **d**  sheet bend

    **e**  clove hitch

    **f**  sheepshank

    **g**  pole hitch

    **h**  slipped hitch

    **i**  halter hitch

    **j**  donkey hitch.

Explain the difference between a knot, a bend and a hitch.

2    Use the knots in Clause 1 and those in Stage 1 to do the following:

    **a**  tie up a parcel

    **b**  hoist a flag

    **c**  shorten a guy rope or washing line that is attached to something at both ends

    **d**  fasten securely a bundle of poles

    **e**  tie up the brailing on a tent.

3    Coil a length of rope.

4 Using square lashing, West Country whipping and other appropriate knots and hitches, do the following:

a make and erect a flag pole using at least two lengths of pole

b make a plaited or Turk's head woggle, a net bag or a cord belt.

## Stage 3

**Hint**

You should choose a suitable weight of string, cord or rope for each knot, bend or hitch.

1 Show that you can tie the following:

a square knot (English)

b hand knot

c chair knot

d true lover's knot

e shamrock knot

f bowline with stopper knot

g sliding figure-of-eight

h double fisherman's knot

i carrick bend

j figure-of-eight hitch

k marline spike hitch

l clove hitch (three ways).

2 Choose from the knots in Clause 1 and those in the earlier stages to do the following:

a make a rope ladder

b fasten a scarf or bow with a fancy knot

c tie a rope securely around another person

65

d make a handline down a slope.

3 Perform three rope tricks.

4 Using square, sheer, snake and tripod lashings, make the following:

a a camp washstand

b a bridge

c a raft.

5 Organise a game or activity for a small group of people that involves a lot of safe knot tying.

## Stage 4

1 Demonstrate the knots, bends, hitches and sinnets that you use in a sport or activity in which you are involved, for example, rock-climbing, handicraft, boating, hairdressing, angling or service preparation. You should use the correct materials and be able to explain:

a why and when a particular knot is used

b the strengths and weaknesses of each knot

c the dangers of incorrect construction and use.

2 **Either**

With a group of people to help you, organise the building of three contrasting pioneering projects.

or

Teach a group of inexperienced knotters the knots, bends and hitches for Stage 1 or 2.

| Stage 1 |
| --- |
| Date..................................... |
| Tester................................... |
| **Stage 2** |
| Date..................................... |
| Tester................................... |
| **Stage 3** |
| Date..................................... |
| Tester................................... |
| **Stage 4** |
| Date..................................... |
| Tester................................... |

# Lifesaver

## Note

Throughout this syllabus the abbreviation RLSS UK has been used for the Royal Life Saving Society of the United Kingdom and ASA for the Amateur Swimming Association.

## Stage 1

### Notes

• If you hold the RLSS UK Rookie Lifeguard 1 Star Core Award for Rescue and do Clause 5, you may have this badge.

• The tester can be any responsible person with relevant, up-to-date knowledge and experience.

1 Know and understand the Water Safety Code.

2 Explain to the tester why a person making a water rescue should put her or his own safety first.

3 Explain to the tester why it is important to give clear instructions to a person whose life is in danger and how you would give a verbal rescue.

4 Demonstrate the following rescues using methods approved by the RLSS UK:

a reaching with a rigid aid

b reaching with an article of clothing

c throwing a rope 3m

d throwing a buoyancy aid 3m.

5 Explain to the tester how to summon the emergency services by telephone and when this should be done.

## Stage 2

### Notes

• If you hold the RLSS UK Rookie Lifeguard Two Star Award, you may have this badge.

• The tester should be either a teacher or examiner of lifesaving or an adult with a current RLSS UK Bronze

Medallion or higher qualification.

1 Know and understand the Water Safety Code.

2 Discuss with the tester the dangers of inland and coastal waters.

3 **Either**

Wearing a T-shirt and shorts or a skirt demonstrate the following personal survival skills:

a a safe entry as for unknown water

b treading water for two minutes

c holding the HELP position for two minutes using a life-jacket or buoyancy aid.

or

Hold ASA Personal Survival 1.

4 Demonstrate (in water) the actions of the following casualties:

a a non-swimmer

b a weak swimmer

c an injured swimmer.

5 Demonstrate the following rescues using methods approved by the RLSS UK:

a Choose appropriate aids and carry out two land-based rescues of a conscious casualty, one being 2m from the water's edge and the other 6m.

b Enter shallow water with a suitable aid and carry out a wading rescue – wade and reach or wade and throw as directed by the tester. Assist the casualty from the water.

Explain to the tester the limitations and dangers of these rescues.

6 Explain the treatment for shock and the procedure for getting medical help.

## Stage 3

**Notes**

• If you hold the RLSS UK Rookie Lifeguard Three Star Award, you may have this badge.

• The tester should be a lifesaving teacher or examiner, or hold a current Award of Merit or higher qualification.

1 Do Clauses 1, 2 and 4 of Stage 2.

2 **Either**

Wearing a long-sleeved shirt and a skirt or trousers demonstrate the following personal survival skills:

a Two safe entries. Explain to the tester when they should be used.

b Treading water for two minutes, one minute waving for help and one minute with both arms in the water.

c The HELP position. Then, with at least two others, take up and hold the 'huddle' for two minutes, using life-jackets or buoyancy aids.

or

Hold the ASA Personal Survival 2.

3 Demonstrate the following rescues using methods

person to land and treat her or him for shock.

**e** Rescue a casualty who is unconscious and floating face down 10m away in deep water. Tow the casualty to shallow water and assess her or his condition. With the help of an adult, safely remove the casualty from the water. Lie the casualty on their back.

approved by the RLSS UK:

**a** Choose from a selection of aids and demonstrate a reaching or throwing rescue of a conscious casualty who may be anywhere between 2 and 8m from the edge of the water. The tester will state the type of casualty.

**b** Enter shallow water and demonstrate a wading rescue of a conscious casualty, using a suitable aid. The tester will state the type of casualty.

**c** Enter shallow water with a suitable aid and demonstrate a non-contact rescue of a casualty 20m away. Accompany the casualty back to safety and assist her or him to land.

**d** Swim 50m to a weak swimmer and conduct a non-contact tow for 50m using an aid of your choice. Assist the

4 Know when and how to use expired air ventilation (EAV). Demonstrate this technique on a manikin and show the tester that you know when and how to summon qualified medical help.

5 With a person acting as the casualty, demonstrate the action you would take if a casualty were to vomit. Place the casualty in the recovery position.

6 Discuss with the tester how a rescuer might feel after an incident.

# L

## Stage 4

### Notes

- If you hold the RLSS UK Bronze Medallion or RLSS UK Rookie Lifeguard Four Star and do Clauses 1 and 4d, you may have this badge.
- Testers should have the following qualifications:
  - Clause 1: RLSS UK teacher or examiner, or Guider with relevant knowledge
  - Clause 2: RLSS UK teacher or examiner, or qualified swimming teacher
  - Clause 3: RLSS UK teacher or examiner
  - Clause 4: RLSS UK teacher or examiner, first aid instructor of a recognised organisation, such as the Red Cross, or qualified doctor/nurse.

1 Present, in an interesting way, water safety knowledge and skills to another Unit in any Section.

2 Either
Wearing a long-sleeved shirt or jumper and a skirt or trousers, demonstrate the following personal survival skills:

a  Enter deep water with a straddle entry.

b  Tread water for two minutes with one arm out of the water to wave for help (you may change arms).

c  Swim 25 m to a floating object.

d  Hold the HELP position for two minutes, then with two others take up the 'huddle' position for a further two minutes.

e  Swim 100 m holding a floating object. Climb out from deep water without using the steps.

Discuss with the tester when these skills might be used.

or

Hold ASA Personal Survival 2.

3 Demonstrate the following rescues using methods approved by the RLSS UK:

a  A land-based rescue of a conscious casualty who may be anywhere between 2 and 10m from the edge. You may choose from a selection of aids.

b  Swim 50m to a conscious casualty who is in deep water. The casualty will attempt to grab you as you approach. Show a reverse and take up the stand-off position. When it is safe to continue conduct a non-contact tow for 50m finishing in deep water in the support position. Assist the casualty to land.

c  Swim 50m to a conscious casualty in deep water and carry out a contact tow over 50m, showing good care of the casualty throughout. Finish in deep water and assist the casualty from the water. Treat her or him for shock.

> **Diving to depths greater than 1.5m may damage your hearing. All diving is undertaken at your own risk.**

Assess the casualty's condition and demonstrate expired air ventilation (EAV) for ten cycles whilst supporting the casualty's body. With the help of an adult, safely remove the casualty from the water. Lie the casualty on their back.

4 This clause may be taken immediately after Clauses 1 to 3 or any time within the following month.

  a Using a manikin, show how you would diagnose a cardiac arrest and demonstrate cardiopulmonary resuscitation (CPR) for at least two minutes, explaining to the tester when you would summon the emergency services.

  b Explain the differences in adult and child EAV and CPR.

  c With a person acting as the casualty, demonstrate the action you would take if a casualty were to vomit.

d Swim 10m and recover an object or dummy from a depth of 1.5m, then substitute the object for a casualty and tow her or him to safety.

Place the casualty in the recovery position.

  d Discuss with the tester why you should summon expert help if you suspect the casualty has a spinal injury.

  e Explain to the tester the treatment you would give to a casualty suffering from bleeding, broken bones, an asthmatic attack or hypothermia.

| **Stage 1** |
| Date................................... |
| Tester................................. |
| **Stage 2** |
| Date................................... |
| Tester................................. |
| **Stage 3** |
| Date................................... |
| Tester................................. |
| **Stage 4** |
| Date................................... |
| Tester................................. |

M

## Music Lover

1   Choose *three* of the following:

- a pop group
- an orchestra
- a brass band
- a string quartet
- a pipe and drum band/marching band
- a steel band
- a jazz group
- a country and western group
- another form of musical group.

Using pictures, tapes, diagrams or other methods, set up a display to show the formation of each group and the type of music played.

2   Over three months keep a diary of the different types of music you have heard. Make comments about them. Which do you prefer and why?

3   Choose three different pieces of music that you have enjoyed. Play them to the tester and tell her or him what you like about them.

| Date ................................. |
| Tester ............................... |
| Comments ......................... |
| ............................................ |
| ............................................ |

# Musician

## Stage 1

1 Play or sing two contrasting pieces.

2 Sing one verse of the National Anthem.

3 Show the tester you can read music by being able to name the lines and spaces in the treble clef, and by clapping a simple rhythm.

4 Make a percussion instrument and, using it, compose a simple percussion accompaniment to a well-known song.

## Stage 2

1 Sing two verses of the National Anthem.

2 Play two contrasting pieces.

3 Make a scrapbook about some aspect of music you really enjoy. Be prepared to discuss this book with the tester. You also may wish to include tapes and/or records.

4 Sing or play at sight simple music provided by the tester.

5 Show that you have used your musical skills for the enjoyment of others.

6 Sustain a second part (either alto or descant) to a tune of your own choice whilst the tester plays the melody.

## Stage 3

1 Prepare a 15 minute musical programme to perform to the tester.

2 Take to the test a composition of about 16 bars in length written by yourself. Be prepared to perform it.

3 Discuss with the tester your playing (or singing) and composition. Consider your choice of repertoire and answer questions on style and expression.

4 Show that you continue to use your musical skills for the enjoyment of others on a regular basis.

5 Discuss with the tester some aspect of music which interests you. Illustrate your discussion with tapes, CDs or records.

| Stage 1 |
| --- |
| Date................................... |
| Tester................................. |
| **Stage 2** |
| Date................................... |
| Tester................................. |
| **Stage 3** |
| Date................................... |
| Tester................................. |

# Needlecraft

## Notes
• At Stages 2, 3, and 4, it is assumed that you can thread a needle and start and finish off the work yourself.

• Items made for one stage must not be presented again at another stage.

## Hint
Commercial paper patterns are expensive, so borrowing and sharing is encouraged (which means that the patterns must be used carefully). Magazines often offer free patterns.

## Stage 1
### Note
• Only one item may be made at school or college.

### Hint
• The type of fabric used, for example, Binca, evenweave or plain cotton, will vary according to your age. Use a needle and thread suitable for the material, for example, tapestry wool, wool, embroidery silk, etc.

1  Show that you can thread a needle and start and finish off your work.

2  Make *two* of the following items:
   • a bookmark
   • a purse
   • a pencil case
   • a book cover (for example, for your Handbook)
   • a beach bag
   • a place mat or something similar.

Decorate both using at least four of the following stitches: chain, stem, blanket, cross, fly, satin, threaded running stitch and whipped running stitch.

## Stage 2
### Note
Only one item may be made at school or college.

1  Show you can tack and hem by sewing a badge onto your uniform or a name tape onto a garment by hand.

2 Use a simple pattern to make a useful article of your choice. You may use a sewing machine. Tell the tester how the pattern was placed on the material.

3 Sew a button by hand onto a garment. Know how to sew on two-hole and four-hole buttons and those with a shank.

4 Make an item of your choice using a different form of needlecraft, for example, tapestry, appliqué (by hand or machine), embroidery, etc. You may not use knitting or crochet.

## Stage 3

### Notes
• Only one item may be made at school or college.

• Your work should show that you can sew by hand and use a sewing machine.

1 Have a working knowledge of a sewing machine.

2 Make a simple garment for yourself and be able to say how you laid the pattern on the fabric and how you made up the garment.

3 Discuss with the tester the importance of the different types, sizes and uses of needles – especially those used at this stage.

4 Make an item for a bedroom (for example, a wall hanging, a cushion cover, a soft toy, a laundry bag, a holdall or a picture) using *one* of the following methods:

• patchwork
• tapestry
• appliqué (by hand or machine)
• soft sculpture
• embroidery (machine, traditional, Hardanger, cross-stitch, etc.)
• bargello.

75

**N**

5 Know what is meant by the International Textile Care Labelling Code and how you would care for the items you have made. Understand the importance of labels in bought items.

## Stage 4

**Notes**

• Only one item may be made at school or college.

• Your work should show a good standard of hand and machine sewing.

1 Know the following:

a the difference between natural and man-made fibres, and how to care for and launder each type

b the suitability of fabrics for different types of garment

c the importance of using the right thread and trimmings for each fabric.

2 Make a garment, using fabric of your choice, from a paper pattern. It should include *at least four* of the following processes:

- two methods of making seams
- neatening raw edges
- disposing of fullness
- finishing a hem
- setting in a sleeve
- making a buttonhole
- setting on a collar
- putting in a zip
- putting in a pocket or applying a patch pocket.

Discuss with the tester the costing and method of making up the garment.

3 Learn a form of needlecraft that you have not used before either in this badge or in any other Interest Badge. Use it to make a useful item for personal or home use.

| | |
|---|---|
| **Stage 1** | |
| Date.................................... | |
| Tester.................................. | |
| **Stage 2** | |
| Date.................................... | |
| Tester.................................. | |
| **Stage 3** | |
| Date.................................... | |
| Tester.................................. | |
| **Stage 4** | |
| Date.................................... | |
| Tester.................................. | |

# Oarswoman

## Stage 1

### Note

The tester should be aged 16 or over and hold The Guide Association Oarsman's permit or have equivalent knowledge and be acceptable to the County Assistant Outdoor Activities Adviser (Boating).

1 Swim 50m and stay afloat for five minutes wearing clothes. This clause may be done in a swimming pool and you may wear a buoyancy aid if you wish.

2 Wear suitable clothing and a buoyancy aid (unless using unclassified water) for the test and be able to explain their importance to the tester.

3 Name the parts of a boat.

4 Demonstrate either by yourself or as one of a crew:

a preparing a boat and launching

b leaving the shore or jetty

c rowing a course, including turning, backing and stopping

d coming alongside a jetty or coming ashore

e putting away a boat and equipment.

5 Demonstrate how to use either a round turn and two half hitches or a bowline for tying up a boat.

6 Understand boat discipline and how to behave towards other water users. Know the rules for meeting, passing and crossing other craft and any local rules about accessing and using the water.

7 Point out any hazards on the water you are using. Know how to call for assistance.

## Stage 2

### Note

If you complete The Guide Association Oarsman Permit, you may have this badge. The syllabus is ▶▶▶

in *Qualifications,* published by The Guide Association.

### Stage 3

**Note**

If you complete The Guide Association Rowing Charge Permit, you may have this badge. The syllabus is in *Qualifications*, published by The Guide Association.

| | |
|---|---|
| **Stage 1** | |
| Date | ................................. |
| Tester | ................................. |
| **Stage 2** | |
| Date | ................................. |
| Tester | ................................. |
| **Stage 3** | |
| Date | ................................. |
| Tester | ................................. |

# Pack Holiday

1 Attend a Pack Holiday from beginning to end.

2 Help to make posters and decorate your Pack Holiday home.

3 Help to prepare and cook a meal.

4 Clear away and wash up after a meal.

5 Make your bed and keep your own things tidy.

6 Make something you could take home from a Pack Holiday.

7 Know how to keep yourself fit and healthy.

8 Make a diary to show what you have done during your Pack Holiday. You may draw or write.

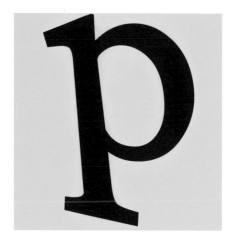

Date .....................................

Tester ...................................

Comments ............................

.............................................

.............................................

79

# Pack Holiday Advanced

## Notes

• Before you take this badge you must have been on one or more Pack Holidays and have spent a total of four or more nights away with your Pack.

• The tester should hold a Pack Holiday Licence.

1 Bring a letter to the test from the Guider-in-Charge of your last Pack Holiday saying that you:

a took part in planning the Pack Holiday (that is, helped to decide on a theme for the holiday, the games to be played and the food to be eaten, prepared charts, wrote a poem or prayer, and took part in other activities)

b kept your own belongings neat and tidy

c helped your Six with the following: serving meals and clearing up afterwards; washing, drying and putting away dishes and cutlery; keeping the area around the Pack Holiday site clean and tidy; preparing and cooking meals; and planning and taking part in prayers.

2 Bring to the test any charts or posters you made before or during the Pack Holiday, and anything you made on Pack Holiday to take home.

3 a Tell the tester what you did on Pack Holiday. You could tell her what you cooked, cleaned, sang and so on.

b Know the Country Code. Explain how you have helped to protect the water, trees, flowers and other living things around the Pack Holiday site.

c Know the Green Cross Code and tell the tester how you kept this whilst on Pack Holiday.

d Know how to keep the Pack Holiday site safe.

e Know how to keep yourself fit and healthy.

4 Bring your own souvenirs of the Pack Holiday to the test. Perhaps you have photographs, craft items, a diary, or things you collected to remind you of where you were and what you did. Talk to the tester about them.

Date ....................................

Tester ....................................

Comments ..........................

....................................................

....................................................

BROWNIE GUIDES

# Pathfinder

p

From your own home or your Pack meeting place:

1   Know the easiest and quickest way of getting to the centre of your neighbourhood and the best way to get to two nearby towns, villages or shopping centres. Know the days when your local shops are closed.

2   Give clear directions, politely and distinctly, to the tester when she or he asks the way to any local places, such as the police station, council offices, post office, toilets, library, church, village hall, chemist's shop, hospital, telephone, garage and petrol station.

3   Visit any interesting place in your neighbourhood, such as a church, castle, abbey or battlefield, and tell the tester about it.

While you are there, look for any difficulties a disabled visitor might encounter and tell the tester about them.

4   Explain to the tester about your local bus or train services. Know how to get to the bus stop or railway station.

Date ...................................

Tester ...................................

Comments ...........................

.............................................

.............................................

81

# Photographer

## Stage 1

1 Tell the tester about your camera and how you use it to take good pictures. You should know the following:

    **a** what size film it takes

    **b** how to load and unload the film

    **c** how to keep your camera clean and remove dust and grit safely.

2 Take 12 prints or transparencies either at a Guide Association event or holiday, or on a chosen theme, for example, animals or landscape. The set of prints must include the following:

    **a** landscapes

    **b** people

    **c** action shots.

The prints should be mounted (as a display or in an album) or presented to show the chosen event or theme clearly to the members of your Six, Patrol or Unit.

## Stage 2

**Note**

When you have been using your camera for six months do Clauses 1, 2 and 3 and choose *one* clause from Clauses 4, 5 or 6.

1 Know how your camera works and be able to explain to the tester its special functions (for example, automatic focus and automatic wind) and how these can help your photography.

2 Know the functions of the different parts of a camera, such as the lens, shutter and stops. Explain briefly how a negative and a positive of a print or transparency are produced.

3 Be able to tell the tester any or all of the following:

a how a lens hood can improve photographs

b the purpose of an ultra-violet or skylight filter

c what camera shake is and how to avoid it

d how to achieve the best angles and lighting to show your subject to the best advantage

e how to avoid 'red eye' when using a flash.

4 Bring to the test a collection of 20 prints taken over a period of six months. They should be mounted as for an exhibition with captions as far as possible. The collection should include the following:

a a sequence of five photographs (which may have been taken at different times) either telling a story or showing different aspects of the subject

b other prints which show at least two of the following subjects: landscape, nature, portrait, architecture, action, backlighting.

Be able to talk about the pictures to your Six, Patrol or Unit.

5 a Make a collection of at least 20 slides covering two of the subjects given in Clause 4b.

b **Either**

Give a slide show to your Six, Patrol or Unit.

or

Have the slides made into prints and exhibit them with captions as described in Clause 4.

6 For the test (which can be taken in your home or anywhere with suitable equipment) show a five-minute video film you have made which demonstrates your understanding of the different techniques required to produce an enjoyable programme. The film may be about:

- a Guiding event or family holiday

- a story with commentary or sound

effects which need not be on the film.

If possible, show the video film to your Six, Patrol or Unit.

## Stage 3

### Note

When you have been using your camera for at least 12 months, mount an exhibiton of photographs or slides, or give a video presentation. Choose and complete Clause 1, 2 or 3.

1 **Black and White and Colour Negative Photography**

a Mount an exhibition of at least ten prints of either different aspects of a single happening or a series of happenings at Guiding events or at a club to which you belong.

b Make sure that the photographs in the exhibition are at least 5 x 7 inches (12.7 x 17.8 cm) and that they have suitable captions for display to the public. At least ►►►

p

half should show some action. All the photographs must have been taken by you and, where possible, developed and printed by you.

c The photographs should illustrate the following subjects: still life, portrait, group, landscape, nature, action.

d Use the appropriate techniques from the following: contre jour, table-top, fill-in-flash, available light.

Discuss your choice with the tester and be prepared to show that you understand the meaning of the techniques you did not use.

2 **Colour Transparencies (Slides)**

a Mount an exhibition of slides suitable for a public meeting, for example, an Annual General Meeting. All the transparencies should have been taken by you, and there should be either a live commentary or a properly recorded and synchronised commentary with suitable music. The requirements are the same as for Clause 1.

b You will be asked to:

• demonstrate how to mount slides.

• explain the advantages and disadvantages of card and glass mounts

• describe the care of both types of mount

• explain the importance of storing slides properly and the results of bad storage.

3 **Video Photography**

a You will be asked to do the following:

• Describe the features you would look for when buying a video camera and why you would need them.

• Explain how to care for your camera and which parts should be regularly cleaned, how they should be cleaned and which parts should not be touched.

• Explain the markings on your camera, for example, F numbers, m, ft, fps, etc., and know how to use them to get the effects you want.

• Know what 'depth of field' means and how to use it.

• Know what LED stands for, what all the LEDs indicate, and what action to take (also on any other equipment you may be using, for example, VCR or projector).

- Explain the essential differences between video and still photography and the cameras used for each, the difficulties a video photographer is likely to face, and the techniques of a good video.

b  Make a video with sound lasting eight to ten minutes. All shooting, editing and production should be by you. Choose *one* of the following themes:

- a documentary on Guiding for public showing

- a record of an event or series of events in your District, Division or County suitable for showing at an Annual General Meeting

- a recruiting film for the Senior Section suitable for showing to Brownies or Guides

- a publicity film about Rangers or Young Leaders suitable for showing to other interested organisations or to the public.

The film must demonstrate at least three of the following techniques: zooming, tilt shot, macro, voice-over and panning to cover landscape. All techniques should be discussed with the tester.

c  Understand the significance of the figures and developing instructions on the film carton and on the cassette or wrapper (for example, ISO Din, C41). Know how to load and unload a 35 mm film and a roll film and what precautions to take.

d  Explain the effects of the following:

- lens hood and filters – black and white as well as colour

- skylight or ultra-violet filters over the lens.

The explanations given should be more detailed than those given in Stage 2, Clause 3.

e  Describe any new ways you may have found of counteracting or minimising camera shake.

| Stage 1 | | |
| --- | --- | --- |
| Date ............................ | | |
| Tester .......................... | | |
| **Stage 2** | | |
| Date ............................ | | |
| Tester .......................... | | |
| **Stage 3** | | |
| Date ............................ | | |
| Tester .......................... | | |

p

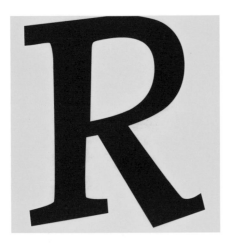

BROWNIE GUIDES

# Radio Communication

1 a  Listen to an amateur radio receiver. Be able to use the tuning dial on the receiver to find different stations.

  b  Write down a few details about the conversations you hear. These could include the date, time, callsign, name of the radio amateur, town or country, and anything you find interesting.

2 a  Spell out loud your first name and home town using the internationally recommended phonetic alphabet.

  b  Listen to simple words the tester spells phonetically and write down or tell the tester what they say.

3  Do *one* of the following:

  • Make a postcard-size QSL (greetings) card for a Brownie radio station.

  • Visit a special event radio station, such as 'Thinking Day on the Air'. Tell the tester what you did there.

  • Write a greetings message that is suitable for sending by radio to another Brownie. It should last about one minute. Include your first name, home town, what you have been doing at Brownies, and a greeting for the other Brownie. Read your message out loud to the tester.

4  Discuss with the tester how two-way radios, such as those used by the police, ships and aeroplanes, can be useful.

Date.....................................

Tester...................................

Comments.............................

...........................................

...........................................

# Rider

## Stage 1

**Note**

If you hold the Pony Club D Test Certificate or the Riding for the Disabled Association Proficiency Test Grade 3 Award, you may have this badge.

1   Show the tester that you know how to dress appropriately and understand the importance of wearing a hard hat.

2   Demonstrate or explain how to:

   **a**   approach a pony or horse correctly, using aids if necessary

   **b**   catch a pony or horse and put on a headcollar/halter

   **c**   lead a pony or horse in hand

   **d**   give a pony or horse an apple or carrot.

3   Be able to:

   **a**   mount and dismount correctly

   **b**   demonstrate the correct position in the saddle and hold the reins correctly

   **c**   ride a quiet pony or horse in an enclosed area without a leading rein and stop, walk, turn and trot safely.

**A rider with a disability should take the test where she is known.**

4   Know how to ride along and across a road with an adult accompanying you.

5   Know the basic needs of a grass-kept pony or horse in summer and winter, for example, feeding, watering and grooming.

6   Identify:

   **a**   the simple points of a pony or horse

   **b**   some parts of a saddle and bridle.

## Stage 2

**Note**

If you hold the Pony Club D Plus Certificate or the Riding for the Disabled Association Proficiency Test Grade 4 Award, you may have this badge.

1   Demonstrate or explain how to control a quiet pony or horse on the road or in the countryside. You should be able to:

   **a**   use simple leg and hand aids effectively

   **b**   make simple turns and circles in walk and trot ►►►

**R**

c  canter over a single pole and a very small fence

d  walk without stirrups

e  alter your stirrups and tighten or loosen your girth while mounted.

2  Show that you understand the Green Cross Code as it applies to riders and the importance of thanking considerate drivers and pedestrians.

3  Know something about caring for your pony or horse. Demonstrate or explain how to:

a  put on a saddle and bridle (with a snaffle bit)

b  clean a saddle and bridle

c  lead a pony or horse in hand at walk and trot

d  tie up a pony or horse correctly

e  pick up and pick out feet.

4  Identify the essential items of a grooming kit and know how they are used.

5  Know the common colours and markings of a pony or horse.

## Stage 3

### Note

If you hold the Pony Club C Test Certificate and complete Clause 11 or hold the Riding for the Disabled Association Proficiency Test Grade 6 Award, you may have this badge.

1  Present yourself and your pony or horse well.

### Riding

2  Show that you can control your mount, have a seat independent of the reins, and maintain the correct position of the hands at walk, trot and canter. You should be able to do the following:

a  use the correct aids to increase and decrease pace; turn circles at walk, trot and canter; canter in a circle on a named leg

b  ride up and down hills and jump low fences in good style

c  trot without stirrups.

3  Understand the care needed when riding in the countryside and across farmland.

### Road Safety

4  Know the Highway Code as it applies to riders and demonstrate an awareness of possible dangers while riding on the roads.

### Stable Management

5  Know how to clean and care for saddlery.

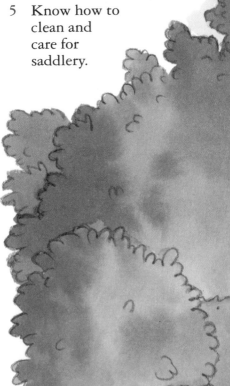

6 Know the main points of feeding and watering ponies or horses and understand the importance of cleanliness.

7 Show that you know how to saddle, bridle and rug up a pony or horse.

8 Understand the care and working of a grass-kept pony or horse.

9 Know when a pony or horse needs shoeing and recognise when it is lame.

10 Know the main indicators for health in a pony or horse and how to treat minor wounds.

**Progress**

11 Keep a record of your stable management and riding activities for three months, noting any improvements.

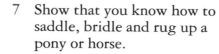

## Stage 4

**Note**

If you hold the Pony Club C Plus Test Certificate and complete Clause 9 or hold the Riding for the Disabled Association Proficiency Test Grade 7 Award, you may have this badge.

### Riding

1 Show that you are a competent rider with a secure seat independent of the reins and understand the correct application of the aids. You should be able to do the following:

a  sitting trot; rising trot on either diagonal; change the diagonal b   ride up and down steep hills and jump fences and ditches at trot and canter

c   change leg at canter through trot

d   open a simple gate without dismounting

e   canter without stirrups.

## Road Safety

2   Show that you understand the Highway Code as it applies to riders and know how to behave when riding in company.

## Stable Management

3   Know how to care for and work both a pony or horse off-grass and a stabled pony or horse. Understand why and how feeding, watering regimes and work have to be varied according to whether the pony or horse is stabled or grass-kept.

4   Know the structure of a pony's or horse's foot. Watch a farrier at work and know the names of the farrier's essential tools.

5   Demonstrate or explain how to fit a saddle and

bridle and understand the importance of well-fitting tack.

6   Recognise and know how to put on a rug, tail bandage, travel bandages and a roller.

7   Know when a pony or horse is lame or in poor condition and be able to recognise minor ailments.

8   Have an understanding of basic first aid and be able to carry out basic treatment for wounds, ailments and lameness as prescribed by a vet.

9   Do *one* of the following and be prepared to talk to the

tester about what you have learned:

• Choose an equestrian sport, for example, show jumping, eventing or dressage. Read a book about it and find out about a sporting personality involved in the sport.

• Build up a scrapbook or file of information on the equestrian subject of your choice.

**Stage 1**
Date...................................
Tester................................

**Stage 2**
Date...................................
Tester................................

**Stage 3**
Date...................................
Tester................................

**Stage 4**
Date...................................
Tester................................

BROWNIE GUIDES

# Road Safety

## Hint

For helpful information contact Sandwell Road Safety Unit, Wigmore, Pennyhill Lane, West Bromwich B71 3RZ.

1 Plot a safe route showing the crossing places for *one* of the following journeys:

- from your home to school
- from your home to the Brownie meeting place
- from a friend's home to your home
- from a friend's home to your school.

Walk your chosen route with the tester.

Date ...................................

Tester ...................................

Comments ...........................

.............................................

.............................................

2 Know the Green Cross Code and explain it.

3 Explain the meaning of the following words: pavement, kerb, vehicle, traffic, pedestrian, stationary car, right of way, T-junction, pelican crossing, zebra crossing, subway and footbridge.

4 Tell the tester how to cross the road using people who help, such as policemen/ policewomen, school crossing patrols, and so on.

5 a Make a collage, poster or leaflet illustrating a safe crossing place, such as a footbridge, subway, pelican crossing, zebra crossing, clear road, etc.

b Know how to walk safely on the road:

- where there is a pavement
- where there is no pavement
- in the dark.

6 Tell the tester what you must do if a stranger starts to talk to you.

R

91

# S

BROWNIE GUIDES

## Safety in the Home

**Hint**

For a safety in the home activity pack contact Tinderbox, PO Box 10, Stourbridge, West Midlands DY9 7YZ.

1 a Give the name, address and telephone number of your family doctor. If you do not know the number, show how you would find it.

  b Show how to make a call on a private telephone and a public telephone.

  c Be able to give someone directions to the public telephone nearest to your house.

  d Know how to call the police, an ambulance or the fire brigade in an emergency according to the situation.

2 Show how you would do the following in a safe way:

  a make a hot milky drink

  b wash and dry sharp knives and carry them to another person

  c strike a match, light a candle and put the matches away.

3 Name an accident which could happen with each of the following:

  a electricity

  b gas

c   solid fuel.

4   Explain one way of
    preventing an accident in
    your house in:
    a   the kitchen
    b   the living room
    c   the bathroom.

5   Tell the tester how the
    following can be
    dangerous to young
    children:
    a   plastic bags
    b   pills and medicines left
        within reach
    c   sharp scissors, needles,
        tins and so on
    d   disinfectants,
        detergents and
        insecticides.

Date....................................

Tester................................

Comments.........................

........................................

........................................

# Science Investigator

**Note**

Keep a record of all your
investigations and be ready to
tell the tester about them.

**Hint**

A pack of activity cards called
*Science and Technology Fun* is
available from The Guide
Association Trading Service,
Guide shops and depots.

1   Carry out all these
    investigations:
    a   Make some plain
        yoghurt. Divide it into
        separate containers and
        find out what happens
        if lemon juice, vinegar
        or bicarbonate of soda
        is added to one portion
        during its preparation.
    b   Grow a broad bean and
        find out what happens
        if it is left in the dark
        and then put in the light.
        If broad beans are not
        available, you can use
        runner
        beans or garden peas
        instead.
    c   Heat some egg white and
        explain how it changes.
    d   Fill some bottles (or
        glasses) with water and
        play a tune.
    e   Use a magnet and find
        out what happens when
        you put it near some
        iron, wood, paper and
        two other substances of
        your choice.

2   Choose and carry out *two*
    projects from this list:
    •   Make a device to measure
        time. Use your device to
        time a job. Tell the tester
        how accurate
        it was.   ▶▶▶

S

- Build an object that will transport a small load (such as a stock cube).
- Make an electric circuit that could be used as a torch.
- Build a tower and find out what load it would support.

3 Choose and carry out *one* of the following:
- Visit a museum or exhibition that is of scientific interest. Tell the tester about your visit.
- Find out about the discoveries of two famous scientists. Tell the tester about their work and how it has affected our lives.

Date.................................

Tester...............................

Comments.........................

...............................................

...............................................

BROWNIE GUIDES

# Seasons

**Note**

Keep your scrapbook and other records in a safe place, as you will need them if you go on to take the Guide Seasons Badge.

1 Make a Seasons Badge scrapbook. Your scrapbook should show the different sorts of weather experienced in your country. It should also show what happens to plants and animals in each of the four seasons.

2 Choose *one* of the following seasons and do all four parts.

**Spring**

a Ask an adult to help you make a nest box. When you have finished it, get permission to put it up in a suitable place.

b Tell your Six or Unit about one folk custom which takes place during the spring.

c Keep a record for at least one month of when and where you see spring flowers, leaves coming on the trees and new baby animals.

d Grow some spring bulbs or corms, such as snowdrops, daffodils or crocuses.

**Summer**

a Make a bird-bath and keep it filled daily with water.

b Know why you should not feed the birds in the summer.

c Keep a record for at least one month of all the birds that you can see. Can you hear them too? Be able to tell the tester about at least one summer visitor (migrant) to this country.

d Watch some butterflies or bees on a flower. Make sure you can tell the tester what they are doing and why.

## Autumn

a  With adult help, collect blackberries or apples and make either a pie or jam.

b  Make a scrapbook of animals which hibernate.

c  Make a collection of autumn leaves. Display them in an interesting way in your scrapbook. Collect some tree seeds, like conkers or acorns, and make some 'fairy furniture' or toy animals from them.

d  Watch a squirrel or some birds eating seeds, fruit or nuts. Put a tree seed, fruit or nut into a pot of soil and leave it for a month. Can you explain what has happened to it at the end of that time?

## Winter

a  Make a bird pudding and feed it to the birds.

b  Tell the tester of at least two ways in which you could help birds or other animals in winter.

c  Keep a record for at least one month of all the birds that visit your bird table. Describe a winter visitor (migrant) to the tester.

d  Grow a bulb, such as a hyacinth, in a clear container or water so that you can see its roots developing.

**S**

Date.....................................

Tester..................................

Comments...........................

..............................................

..............................................

95

## Short Tennis 1

Practise and complete these six starter skills:

a   run 'n' balance
b   drop 'n' bounce
c   toss 'n' bounce
d   aim 'n' throw
e   throw 'n' rally
f   drop 'n' hit.

Date ...............................

Tester ............................

Comments ......................

..............................................

..............................................

## Short Tennis 2

**Note**

The maximum age for playing short tennis is ten years.

Practise and complete these six bat 'n' ball skills:

a   feed 'n' catch – forehand
b   feed 'n' catch – backhand
c   underarm serve
d   overarm serve
e   forehand volley
f   backhand volley.

Date ...............................

Tester ............................

Comments ......................

..............................................

..............................................

## Sight Awareness

**Hint**

The Royal National Institute for the Blind (RNIB) Head Office is at 224 Great Portland Street, London W1N 6AA. Look in the telephone directory for the address and telephone number of your local organisation.

### Stage 1

1   Make a collage or sculpture which a blind or partially-sighted person can handle and describe. Try to use materials which will feel interesting.

2   Find out and tell the tester about guide dogs for the blind and how they are trained.

3   Identify six objects correctly by touch and six by smell.

4   Explain how to approach and introduce yourself to

a blind or partially-sighted person.

## Stage 2

1  Make a short recording of at least three stories or articles you would like to share with a blind person of your own age.

2  Know something of the work of *one* of the National Voluntary Organisations which serve the needs of blind or partially-sighted people, such as:

- British Talking Book Service
- Royal National Institute for the Blind
- Sense.

Share this information with members of your Unit.

3  Take part in a game or activity in your Unit wearing either a blindfold or a pair of covered glasses.

4  Tell the tester about the different coloured canes, their use and meaning, and find your way around a room blindfolded but with the aid of a cane.

## Stage 3

1  Using an alphabet card if necessary, read a message in Grade 1 Braille and write in your Promise using a Braille Frame and Stylus so that a third person may read it.

2  Find out something about a famous blind person, for example, Louis Braille, Helen Keller, Laura Bridgeman, Arthur Sculthorpe or David Blunkett MP, and tell

the tester what you have learned.

3  Find out about local organisations/facilities for the blind, for example, talking newspapers, sports associations, scented gardens.

4  List three hazards that a person may encounter because of their sight loss and what safety devices are available to help, for example, around pedestrian crossings, cooker knobs and liquid level indicators.

5  Know the best way to 'guide' a blind person. Lead a blindfolded partner and show how to guide that person to a chair.

6  Describe the shape and contents of a room so that a blind or blindfolded person can safely negotiate her or his way around it.

## Stage 4

1  Learn the deafblind alphabet and use it to introduce yourself. Teach the deafblind ▶▶▶

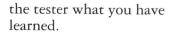

97

alphabet to a group and design some activities to practise its use.

2 Find out about the history of aids for improving vision, for example, glasses, contact lenses, and the causes and treatment of blindness.

3 Find out what it is like to be blind or partially sighted by talking to someone with this disability. Find out how they overcome some of the difficulties they encounter and explain this to the tester.

4 Experience for yourself what it is like to be led by a person, using the 'Sighted Guide' technique, while your vision is artificially impaired.

5 Make or adapt a game for a child with a vision impairment.

6 **Either**
Design something which will enable a blind person to become more independent.

or

Learn 'Sighted Guide' skills and, for approximately ten minutes, be able to guide the tester safely round a route chosen together, using appropriate strategies to overcome any problems. The route should include:

a crossing a road

b steps or stairs

c a doorway

d reaching for an object.

---

**Stage 1**

Date....................................

Tester..................................

**Stage 2**

Date....................................

Tester..................................

**Stage 3**

Date....................................

Tester..................................

**Stage 4**

Date....................................

Tester..................................

---

BROWNIE GUIDES

# Signaller

**Hint**

For further information please send a stamped addressed envelope to Youth Activities, The Guide Association, 17–19 Buckingham Palace Road, London SW1W 0PT.

1 Out of talking range, send and read short messages in semaphore or Morse.

2 Know the following procedure signals:

a calling up (sender)

b go ahead (reader)

c I have the word (reader)

d end of message (sender)

e message received (reader).

If you make a mistake, know how to cancel your message:

a erase (sender)

b answered by C (reader).

Date.................................

Tester..............................

Comments........................

.........................................

.........................................

# Speaker

## Note

In group work at all stages, you should show that you are able to listen and respond in a relevant way to other people. Speech should be audible and, if a microphone is necessary, you should know how to use it correctly.

## Stage 1

1 Tell the tester about one of your hobbies or about an interesting experience you have had.

2 Take part in a group discussion, for example, to plan something.

3 Recite or read aloud a poem or short prose passage of your choice.

4 Thank someone for something they have done for you or given to you.

5 Ask permission for something.

6 Listen to a verbal message and then repeat it to someone.

## Stage 2

1 Give a prepared informal talk (using notes if you want) to a group about a hobby or interesting experience.

2 Take part in a group discussion, for example, to plan something, and then report the arguments and conclusion to someone.

3 Either
Read aloud a passage of your choice from the writings of your faith.

or

Lead prayers.

4 Introduce two people to each other using normal conventions.

5 Know how to introduce a guest speaker.

6 Give a clear explanation or directions, for example, of

S

**S**

how to do something or how to get somewhere.

## Stage 3

1 Give a prepared informal talk (using notes if you want) on a topic that interests you. The talk should show a clear structure. You should be prepared to answer questions on it afterwards and to describe how you would use visual aids, including an overhead projector, to illustrate your talk.

2 Take part in *one* of the following activities or something similar:
- a radio game, for example, 'Just a Minute'
- a hat debate
- a balloon debate.

3 Read aloud a passage of your choice that was written for a particular purpose, for example, to persuade or to amuse.

4 Chair an informal discussion.

5 Be able to give a vote of thanks.

6 Explain the techniques of speaking to less experienced speakers, for example, the need to vary intonation and the use of pauses, pitch, stress, pace, gesture and eye contact. Where possible, demonstrate how it should be done.

## Stage 4

1 Give a prepared formal talk (using notes if you want), lasting four to six minutes, on a subject on which there is more than one point of view. If you like, you can argue a line of thought or you can discuss the various approaches.

2 Speak in a formal debate.

3 Read aloud or recite two contrasting passages of your choice and use suitable voice techniques for each.

4 Chair a formal discussion or debate and describe the duties of a chairperson.

5 Explain the following terms:
- a proposition
- b opposition
- c point of information
- d point of order
- e motion.

6 Listen to, or watch, a parliamentary debate and discuss with the tester some of the techniques used by the speakers.

**Stage 1**

Date.................................

Tester..............................

**Stage 2**

Date.................................

Tester..............................

**Stage 3**

Date.................................

Tester..............................

**Stage 4**

Date.................................

Tester..............................

# Sportswoman

**Note**

You may hold more than one Sportswoman Badge if you are tested on more than one sport.

1  **a** Choose the sport you want to be tested in. This may be a team, individual, combat or racquet sport.

   **b** Record how you are going to improve over a six-week period. This may be through gaining an award or improving your skills.

2 Show that you have taken an active part in your chosen sport over a period of six weeks and improved as recorded.

3 Be able to discuss with the tester the rules and regulations of your chosen sport, including any safety aspects.

Date.....................................

Tester.................................

Comments.........................

.............................................

.............................................

# Stargazer

1 With an adult you know, have a session out-of-doors at night to look at the stars. Find the North Star and the Plough. (Where appropriate, the Southern Cross should be substituted for the North Star.)

2 Look at the stars through a telescope or field glasses. If you can, visit a planetarium or an observatory.

3 Point out two constellations in the sky

▶▶▶

other than the Plough and know their stories.

4 Tell the tester about the phases of our moon.

5 Find out something about three planets in our solar system.

6 Know why sailors in ancient times needed to know about the stars.

Date.............................

Tester............................

Comments......................

.......................................

.......................................

# Survival

### Note
At all stages, the test should (as much as possible) be based on practical tasks rather than theory. Suitable clothing should always be worn.

### Hint
For further information refer to:

• *Improve Your Survival Skills* by Lucy Smith, published by Usborne.

• *Survival: A Complete Guide to Staying Alive* by Martin Forrester, published by Sphere.

### Stage 1

1 Make an emergency shelter. (You may ask someone to help you but you should give the instructions.)

2 Demonstrate or describe a way of collecting water, for example, a solar still.

3 Recognise three edible and three inedible plants. (You may do this from pictures if you wish.)

4 Show how to find north with a compass.

5 Follow a trail of 0.8 to 1.6 km (0.5 to 1 mile), depending on the locality. The trail may be of woodcraft signs, human or animal tracks, secret clues, etc. The tester may go with you.

6 Demonstrate or describe two methods of survival swimming.

7 Describe what you should do if you become snowbound in a car.

### Stage 2

1 Demonstrate or explain the factors that should be considered when choosing and designing a site for an overnight shelter.

2 Know when and why water might need to be purified and demonstrate or explain two ways of doing this.

3 Gather wood, light a fire and cook a two-course meal.

4 Show how to find north without a compass.

5 Remain in the open for half an hour, moving as little as possible, and observe the animal, bird, insect and plant life going on around you. Describe this to the tester, saying what, if anything, would be useful for survival.

6 Know which garments to discard and which to retain when immersed in cold water in an emergency.

7 Know how to prevent, recognise and treat hypothermia. Describe the early signs of extreme weather conditions.

## Stage 3

1 Either
Build a shelter that would stand up to wet and windy conditions for at least two nights.

or

Build (or explain how to build) a snowhole.

2 Describe four different ways in which you might find water for survival.

3 Demonstrate or describe two different ways of lighting a fire without matches. Explain which woods are good and which are unsuitable for lighting a fire. Light a fire and cook a two-course meal without utensils.

4 Demonstrate how you would take a compass bearing and convert it to a map for *two* of the following purposes:

- to identify a peak or some other geographical feature
- to work out your position through a resection
- to take the aspect of a slope to work out your position.

5 Describe at least three methods of attracting the attention of rescuers.

6 Know what to do in a car that has sunk under water.

7 Explain the importance of the following in cold weather conditions:

a food

b drink

c alcohol

d hygiene

e breathing through the nose.

## Stage 4

1 Prepare an emergency survival kit. Explain to the tester why you have chosen each item and how it could be used.

2 Know how to use and maintain an axe and saw.

3 Describe what you would do if you were lost in:

a a forest

b mist in open country.

4 Do *one* of the following:

- Train one or more girls in the ▶▶▶

skills and knowledge necessary to pass Stage 1, 2 or 3.

- Set up an incident hike or survival trail for a group less experienced than yourself to follow.

- Negotiate with the tester a personal challenge that will test your resourcefulness and preparedness. (This could be undertaken with a group.)

---

**Stage 1**

Date .................................

Tester .................................

**Stage 2**

Date .................................

Tester .................................

**Stage 3**

Date .................................

Tester .................................

**Stage 4**

Date .................................

Tester .................................

---

# Swimmer

**Note**

The abbreviation STA has been used for the Swimming Teachers' Association and ASA for the Amateur Swimming Association.

## Stage 1

**Note**

The tester should be a qualified swimming teacher, your regular swimming teacher or a suitably experienced adult.

1 Either

  a Safely jump in from the edge of a pool.

  b Bending your knees, submerge yourself in shallow water ten times, breathing out each time.

  c Briefly sit on the bottom of the pool. Sculling is permitted.

  d Push off from the side of the pool, showing a back glide, and regain the standing position.

  e Swim dog-paddle or front crawl for 10m.

  f Swim on your back for 10m.

  g Swim either front crawl, back crawl or breast stroke for 10m.

or

Hold the STA Pool Frog 2 Award.

2 Discuss with your Guider the hygiene and safety rules to be followed when using a swimming pool.

## Stage 2

**Note**

The tester should be a qualified swimming teacher.

1 Either

  a Jump in to deep water and tread water for 20 seconds.

  b Scull in a sitting tuck position for 20 seconds,

stretch out to a back float and then regain a standing position.

c   With your body in a vertical position and your feet together, scull with your hands and keep your mouth clear of the water for five seconds.

d   Float on your back with your feet together for two minutes, scull with your hands to stay afloat.

e   With a float, swim front crawl, legs only, for 15 m.

f   With your hands behind your head, swim back crawl, legs only, for 15 m.

g   Using a float, swim breast stroke, legs only, for 15 m.

h   Swim either breast stroke, front crawl or back crawl for 25 m.

or

Hold the STA Pool Frog 3 Award.

2   Swim 50 m confidently and without pause, any stroke.

3   Discuss with your Guider the reasons for hygiene and safety rules at your regular swimming place.

## Stage 3

### Notes

• If you hold the ASA Bronze Challenge or Scottish Speedo Swimming Award equivalent, you may omit Clause 2.

• For the first choice in Clause 2, the tester should be a qualified swimming teacher. For the second choice in Clause 2, the tester should be a responsible adult with the relevant knowledge and experience.

> **Diving to depths greater than 1.5 m may damage your hearing. Diving is undertaken at your own risk.**

1   Discuss with your tester or Guider the accidents that could occur if people disregard the safety rules at your regular swimming pool and at fun pools.

Either

2   a   Jump into deep water.
    b   Swim 10 m followed by a surface dive and an underwater swim of 5 m.

**c** Tread water in a vertical position for three minutes.

**d** Scull, head first, feet still and near the surface, for 15m.

**e** Swim 400m using two strokes, with at least 100m using one of the strokes. Climb out of the deep end without using the steps.

or

**a** Swim regularly for three months. Make or get a swim-fit card from your local pool and keep a record of the distances you swim. Show this to the tester.

**b** Challenge yourself to a 600m swim, making a note of the time it takes you to complete this. Aim to swim 600m in less time than before. Keep a record of the dates and times taken and show this to the tester.

**c** At the test:

• Without pausing, swim 200m using one stroke and then swim a further 200m using a different stroke.

• Tread water for two minutes.

## Stage 4

**Notes**

• If you hold the ASA Gold Challenge Award or the Scottish Speedo Swimming Award equivalent, you may omit Clause 2.

• The tester should be a qualified swimming teacher, except for Clause 1, which should be assessed and signed for by the adult involved, for example, a club organiser or Unit Guider.

> **Diving to depths greater than 1.5m can damage your hearing. Diving is undertaken at your own risk.**

1 Choose *one* of the following:

- Under adult supervision, assist a non-swimmer to gain more experience in the swimming pool on at least three separate occasions within a two-month period.

- Help at a swimming club or disabled swimming sessions on a regular basis for at least two months.

- Give an interesting presentation of swimming to another Unit from any Section. Your presentation should include the following aspects: fun, health, sociability, safety and skills.

2 **Either**

a Safely dive or straddle entry into deep water (1.8m minimum depth) and swim 100m in two minutes using two different strokes with 50m of each.

b Tread water for three minutes with one hand raised above your head.

You may change hands if necessary.

c Scull head first on your back for 10m, tuck, rotate 360° and return, sculling feet first.

d Swim 10m, perform a forward somersault without touching the pool floor and continue swimming for a further 10m in the same direction.

e In 25 minutes, swim 800m (at least 200m for each stroke) using three of the following: front crawl, back crawl, breast stroke, butterfly, Old English backstroke or side stroke.

f Climb out without assistance.

*or*

a Swim regularly and discuss personal swimming goals with your Guider/teacher/ coach and, together, set yourself three new targets to achieve over the next three months.

Show the tester records of this.

b At the test show the following skills:

- Safely dive or straddle entry into deep water (1.8m minimum) and swim 600m using three different strokes.

- Tread water for four minutes.

- Retrieve an object from a depth of 1.5m.

- Climb out without using the steps.

**S**

| Stage 1 |
| Date................................... |
| Tester................................ |
| **Stage 2** |
| Date................................... |
| Tester................................ |
| **Stage 3** |
| Date................................... |
| Tester................................ |
| **Stage 4** |
| Date................................... |
| Tester................................ |

# T

## Thrift

1 Find out what the word thrift means.

2 **Either**
Make something new out of something old.

*or*

Make something useful out of bits you would normally throw away.

3 Show how wisely you have used your own money over four weeks.

4 Save newspapers, postage stamps, bottle tops or greetings cards for at least three months to help a charity. Find out about your chosen charity and discover what happens to the things you have saved.

5 Tell the tester of five ways you could be thrifty at home.

Date ...................................

Tester ...................................

Comments ...................................

...................................

...................................

## Toymaker

**Note**

All your toys should be well made, safe and ready for use before you show them to the tester.

Make *three* of the toys from this list:

- A toy from materials which would otherwise be thrown away.
- A simple puppet using any suitable material. (You could make a glove puppet, two finger puppets, a shadow puppet, a jointed puppet, or something similar.) Show how you would bring the puppet to life.

- **Either**
  A set of doll's furniture for yourself.

  **or**

  A Brownie scene for your Six home. (You should use cardboard, matchboxes or any other strong materials to make this toy and the base for the Brownie scene should measure 30cm x 23cm.)
- A toy of your own choice which is different from the other things you have made.

- A well-arranged, clean scrapbook as a special Good Turn for a child or adult who is in hospital.

Date ...................................

Tester ...............................

Comments .........................

....................................................

....................................................

109

# W

## Walking

**Notes**

• Adults will need to accompany you or supervise you on the walks as appropriate. The tester should be approved by the Division Commissioner.

• The definitions of the four categories of countryside for which the Walking Safely Training Scheme provides training can be found in *The Guiding Manual* and *Qualifications,* both published by The Guide Association.

• Details of your walks can be recorded in *The Walking Safely Training Scheme Record Book,* published by The Guide Association.

### Stage 1

1   Show the tester that you know how to dress to go on a walk. Be able to show your bag or rucsac and what you carry with you.

2   Go on four walks, one of which should be at least 5 km (3 miles) in length. Make a brief record of each walk to include:

   a   the date

   b   the weather

   c   where you went.

You may use any method (such as photos, drawings, postcards, a tape or a play) to record the walk.

3   Know the eight points of the compass and show the

tester where North is marked on simple maps.

4  Show that you understand the Green Cross Code and the Country Code. To do this you may devise a play or draw a chart, etc. in your group.

5  Go for a short walk with the tester. You can plan this with the tester and anybody else being tested. Talk about interesting things you see on the way.

## Stage 2

1  Be able to show the tester that you have thought about clothes and footwear for walks in different kinds of weather and area. Show what you would pack in your rucsac.

2  Make up a simple first aid kit. Know how to treat cuts, grazes, stings, blisters and sprains. Be aware of the effects of the sun.

3  Go on at least five walks, one of which should not be less than 10 km (6 miles) in length.

Make a simple record of:

a  where you went

b  who was in the group

c  the date and weather

d  the distance covered

e  the purpose of the walk

f  the time taken

g  anything interesting.

4  Show a basic understanding of how a Silva compass works and be able to walk along simple bearings.

5  With the tester and others to be tested, plan a route using suitable maps. These might have a scale of 1:50,000 or 1:25,000, or be local sketch maps. Show your ability to follow a section of the maps. While you are on the walk, show an understanding of relevant Green Cross, Country and Water Safety Codes.

## Stage 3

1  Show the tester your clothing and footwear, and be able to explain why you chose those particular items. Also show your

waterproofs, personal first aid kit, emergency rations and emergency equipment. Tell the tester when and how you would use these.

2  Demonstrate your knowledge of first aid.

a  Know how to deal with choking.

b  Be able to deal with grazes, stings, sprains and the effects of heat.

c  Understand when not to move a casualty and when to call for extra help.

3  Participate in at least six walks, one of which should be no less than 15 km (9 miles) in length and one, if possible, should be to a height of 350 m. Explain the purpose of each walk to the tester. Keep a record of the walks and include:

a  a description of the route

b  a route card to show distance and timing

c  the OS number of the map used

**d** details of the group

**e** emergency procedures, such as escape routes and telephone numbers.

4 Demonstrate your map skills.

   **a** Be able to give six-figure grid references from a 1:25,000 or 1:50,000 map, and show an understanding of the symbols used.

   **b** Set the map using a Silva compass and features. Be able to tell the tester the direction of different features in relation to others (grid bearings).

5 Using a 1:25,000 or 1:50,000 map, prepare a route card showing grid reference, height, distance, estimated timing and escape route. With a group, take the tester on this route (or meet her/him along it). The route should be at least 12km (7 miles) long in Medium country or above (possibly valley bottoms in Difficult country).

### Stage 4

1 Bring to the test correct clothing and equipment, including emergency gear, for Medium to Difficult country.

2 Demonstrate your knowledge of first aid.

   **a** Demonstrate artificial respiration.

   **b** Demonstrate pulmonary resuscitation.

   **c** Be able to put someone in the recovery position.

   **d** Recognise the signs and symptoms of hypothermia and know how to deal with the situation.

   **e** Explain how to deal with choking.

   **f** Know when it is necessary to request emergency help and how much first aid you yourself should give.

3 Keep a record of the walks that you have completed.

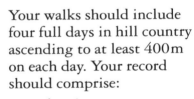

Your walks should include four full days in hill country ascending to at least 400m on each day. Your record should comprise:

**a** a sketch map, description or copy of the route

**b** an account of the purpose of the walk

**c** the route card

**d** notes on the walk, including date and weather conditions

**e** observations of land use, vegetation, geology, etc.

4  At the test, prepare a route card to include the following: grid reference, height, distance, magnetic bearings, alternative routes and timing. Use the card to demonstrate your ability to find your way in unknown country, using a map and compass.

5  Using either a 1:50,000 or a 1:25,000 map – or both – point out to the tester land forms commonly associated with upland areas and explain their significance to the hill walker. Repeat this exercise on the ground, as far as possible.

6  Know the Country Code and Water Safety Code and read *Safety on Mountains,* produced by the British Mountaineering Council and available from The Guide Association Trading Service. Explain to the tester the following:

a  How the hill walker can contribute to the conservation of upland areas and understand the importance of public rights of way, permissive paths, access land and the reasons for restrictions.

b  How to obtain information about an area, including local weather forecasts and information about rescue posts.

c  The effect that physical features might have on weather conditions, group morale and speed of travel.

---

**Stage 1**
Date .................................
Tester ...............................
**Stage 2**
Date .................................
Tester ...............................
**Stage 3**
Date .................................
Tester ...............................
**Stage 4**
Date .................................
Tester ...............................

---

# Water Safety

**Note**
The abbreviation RLSS UK has been used throughout this syllabus for the Royal Life Saving Society of the United Kingdom.

### Stage 1
**Notes**
• If you hold the RLSS UK Rookie Lifeguard Two Star Core Award for Water Safety, you may have this badge.

• The tester may be any responsible adult with relevant, up-to-date knowledge.

1  Explain why water outside (for example, lakes, rivers, canals and ponds) can be dangerous.

2  Explain why shallow water can be dangerous.

3  Explain why cold water can be dangerous.

4  Show an understanding of safety signs and flags.

5  Discuss locations where people could drown.

6  Explain where the safest places to swim are and why.

7  Explain why you must never swim alone.

8  Know the Water Safety Code.

9  Be aware of the different causes of water pollution.

## Stage 2

**Notes**
- If you hold the RLSS UK Rookie Lifeguard Three Star Core Award for Water Safety and do Clause 6, you may have this badge.
- The tester should be a person holding a current lifesaving award, a lifesaving teacher, a swimming teacher or a responsible adult with relevant, up-to-date knowledge and experience.
- All parts of this badge may take place on dry land, including Clause 6. You may

take this badge even if you cannot swim.

1  Know and understand the Water Safety Code.

2  Name *two* possible dangers involving water at each of the following locations:
- gardens
- parks and boating pools
- swimming pools
- farms and countryside
- rivers, canals and streams
- reservoirs and lakes
- beaches.

3  Discuss with the tester the problems of water pollution and water-borne diseases. What precautions can you take?

4  Explain why swimmers are more likely to drown than non-swimmers.

5  Choose *one* of the following:
- Give a five-minute presentation on water safety to your Unit.
- Produce a water-safety booklet for your Unit.
- Design and make a water-safety poster and display it at your meeting place, school or library.

6  Demonstrate the following rescues using methods approved by the RLSS UK:

a  reaching with a rigid aid

b  reaching with an article of clothing

c  throwing a rope 5 m to a person

d  throwing a buoyancy aid 5 m to a person.

Show and explain how to keep yourself safe while conducting these rescues.

| Stage 1 | |
|---|---|
| Date | ................................. |
| Tester | ................................. |
| **Stage 2** | |
| Date | ................................. |
| Tester | ................................. |

# Windsurfer

## Stage 1

**Notes**

• If you hold an RYA National Windsurfing Scheme Level 1 or an RYA Junior Windsurfing Scheme Level 1 and complete Clause 1, you may have this badge.

• The tester for Clauses 2 to 5 should be an experienced windsurfer over the age of 16. This person may also test Clause 1.

1 Swim 50m and stay afloat for five minutes wearing clothes. This may be done in a swimming pool and you may wear a buoyancy aid if you wish.

2 Wear suitable clothing and a buoyancy aid. Explain to the tester why these are important.

3 Carry and launch the board and rig separately and raise the rig (with assistance if required).

4 Sail the board across wind, upwind and downwind. Do 180° turn, basic tacking and gybing. Stop the board.

5 Dismantle the rig while afloat, roll it up and paddle back to shore.

## Stage 2

**Notes**

• If you hold an RYA Junior Windsurfing Scheme Level 2 or an RYA National Windsurfing Scheme Level 2 and do Clause 1, you may have this badge.

• The tester for Clauses 2 to 8 should be an experienced windsurfer approved by the County Assistant Outdoor Activities Adviser (Boating).

1 Swim 50m and stay afloat for five minutes wearing clothes. This may be done in a swimming pool and you may wear a buoyancy aid if you wish.

2 Wear suitable clothing and a buoyancy aid. Be able to discuss your choice with the tester.

3 Name the main parts of the board. Rig a board demonstrating the use of knots and a safety leash.

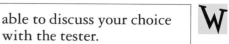

▶▶▶

4  Show that you can, with assistance if required, launch the board and rig connected at the water's edge, get onto the board in shallow water and sail away, return to shore in control, and remove the board from the water.

5  Sailing a set triangular course in winds of at least 8 knots, show an awareness of the three basic 'rules of the road' and that you are competent in the following techniques:

   a  steering using body weight and rig

   b  altering the daggerboard

   c  sail adjustment, board balance and trim

   d  tacking

   e  gybing.

6  Know, and if possible demonstrate, how to be towed by another windsurfer and by a safety boat.

7  Describe five methods of self rescue and demonstrate two. Know the distress signal.

8  Be able to explain the 'seven common senses' and how you would choose a safe sailing area, taking into account cover wind direction, water state, tides, Beaufort scale and personal limitations.

## Stage 3

**Notes**

• If you hold an RYA Junior Windsurfing Scheme Level 3 or an RYA National Windsurfing Scheme Level 3 and complete Clause 1, you may have this badge.

• The tester for Clauses 2 to 4 should be an RYA Windsurfing Instructor or hold a qualification approved by the County Assistant Outdoor Activities Adviser (Boating). This person may also test Clauses 1 and 5.

1  Swim 50m and stay afloat for five minutes wearing clothes. This may be done in a swimming pool and you may wear a buoyancy aid if you wish.

2  Present yourself for the test wearing suitable clothing and a buoyancy aid, and show that you can check whether equipment is safe and suitable. Explain how you would choose a safe sailing area and show a knowledge of local conditions and hazards.

3  Demonstrate that you are competent in the following techniques:

## Rigging

**a** Rig various types of sail, with assistance if required, and know in which order to de-rig.

**b** Know the types of harness line available.

**c** Know how to position and adjust harness lines.

**d** Know the correct adjustment of footstraps.

## Launching, Starting and Landing

**e** Carry and launch a rig, assembled with assistance if required.

**f** Beach start in stronger winds and control the board in shallows.

**g** Uphaul a rig and start in stronger winds.

**h** Come ashore under control and land in stronger winds.

**i** Know how to care for equipment ashore and afloat.

## Sailing Techniques and Stance

**j** Demonstrate correct harness adjustment.

**k** Hook in and out in stronger winds.

**l** Know the efficient planing stance when hooked in.

**m** Know the basic footstrap technique (getting in and out of at least one).

**n** Know the beginnings of footsteering with daggerboard retracted.

**o** Be aware of the purpose of a mast track and how to adjust it.

**p** 'Rail' upwind.

## Manoeuvres

**q** Tack in stronger winds.

**r** Gybe in stronger winds with daggerboard up.

## Freestyle

**s** Demonstrate three freestyle manoeuvres.

## Rescue

**t** Demonstrate being towed in stronger winds.

**u** Know, and if possible demonstrate, how to tow a board with rig and person.

**4** Know how to deal with emergency situations – self-help and getting help.

**5** Know how to recognise and deal with hypothermia. Demonstrate how you would:

**a** stop bleeding

**b** identify and treat a broken bone

**c** treat an unconscious breathing patient.

Using a manikin, show how to give expired air resuscitation.

| Stage 1 | |
| --- | --- |
| Date.................................... | |
| Tester.................................. | |
| **Stage 2** | |
| Date.................................... | |
| Tester.................................. | |
| **Stage 3** | |
| Date.................................... | |
| Tester.................................. | |

BROWNIE GUIDES

# World Cultures

**Note**

To gain this badge you should complete *five* clauses. If you pass five more clauses, you may have another World Cultures Badge.

**Hint**

You will find lots of activities and information in *A World of Ideas,* published by The Guide Association.

1 Make a 'time capsule' or collection of objects that show your home life and/or Brownie life. Show it to your Unit and then store or bury it.

2 List or draw some of the food that you have eaten during the past week. Label which items have come from different parts of the world.

3 Cut out pictures from magazines or newspapers showing girls/women doing different things around the world. Use these pictures to show what jobs girls/women do.

4 Make a decoration from another country, for example, Mexican god's eye, Danish heart, Swedish dove, Rangoli patterns, etc.

5 Listen to or read a story from another country, then act it out with your Six.

6 Do *one* of the following:
- Make and/or decorate eggs as they do for Easter in some countries in Europe.
- Make St Nicholas biscuits (as made in Scandinavia for Christmas).
- Make honey cake which is eaten at Jewish New Year.

7 Help plan and take part in a Japanese doll festival or Chinese New Year celebration.

8 Make a mask of an animal from another part of the world or a mask to represent a custom or tradition other than your own.

9 Jewellery from other countries is often made of natural objects. Make ear-rings or a necklace using natural materials, or use modelling clay to simulate bone or teeth.

10 Find out about various kinds of clothes from different countries of the world and make a collection which may include pictures, costume dolls or clothes.

11 **Either**
Play a singing game from another country.

or

Make a musical instrument from another country.

12 Make a model of a house from another country and find out what it would be built from.

Date ...................................

Tester ...................................

Comments ...........................

...............................................

...............................................

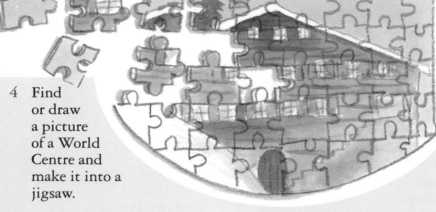

BROWNIE GUIDES

# World Guiding

**Note**

To gain this badge you should complete *five* clauses. If you pass five more clauses, you may have another World Guiding Badge.

**Hint**

You will find lots of activities and information in *A World of Ideas*, published by The Guide Association.

1  Sing a Brownie song from another country.

2  Make a friendship circle of paper dolls. Colour each one with a different Brownie uniform from around the world.

3  Find out what WAGGGS stands for. Wear the World Badge and tell somebody what it means.

4  Find or draw a picture of a World Centre and make it into a jigsaw.

5  Make a badge using the symbol from one of the World Centres.

6  Send a tape, letter or picture to a Brownie in another country. You could either do this on your own or with your Unit.

7  Take part in an event or activity with another Unit. Say 'hello' to a Brownie you don't know and give her something you have made.

8  Cook and taste something that a Brownie in a Commonwealth country might eat.

9  Design a Thinking Day card and send it to someone you know in Guiding.

10  Help plan and take part in a Thinking Day celebration.

11  Talk with an adult you know, who was a Brownie. What was it like to be a Brownie when she was your age?

12  Choose a country that has Brownies, make a poster, and use it to tell your Six about these Brownies.

Date.....................................

Tester..................................

Comments............................

...........................................

...........................................

BROWNIE GUIDES

# World Issues

**Note**

To gain this badge you should complete *five* clauses. If you pass five more clauses, you may have another World Issues Badge.

**Hint**

You will find lots of activities and information in *A World of Ideas,* published by The Guide Association.

1 Plant a tree in your local area. Why are trees important to the air we breathe? Where are trees in danger?

2 Take some cans or bottles to a recycling unit or collect some newspapers or clothes for recycling. Find out how they will be recycled.

3 Taste different types of clean safe water, such as tap water, filtered water, bottled water, etc. Do they taste any different? Which do you prefer? Make a list

or draw pictures of everything you use water for in one day.

4 Draw the flag or symbol of an organisation that helps people across the world. How could you support the organisation?

5 Help plan and take part in a mini Olympic Games or Winter Olympics. Where are the next Olympics being held?

6 Face a partner. Work out three ways in which you are different and three ways in which you are the same. How important are the differences? Can you think of three things you have in common with Brownies in other countries?

7 Choose something, used a lot in your home or at Pack Holiday, that is grown overseas, for example, tea, coffee, bananas, pineapple,

etc. Make something to eat or drink using this food.

8 Find a photograph in a newspaper or magazine of something happening in another country. Make up a story about the photograph. This can be written, taped, presented as a cartoon, acted, etc.

9 Make up a short play about people arguing and then try

not to argue with anyone for a week. How many arguments did you have? What were they about?

10 In a group, without speaking, create a giant machine. Each Brownie can act as one part of it. What is its purpose? How did you communicate?

11 Show someone that you can wash your hands and clean your teeth properly. What could happen to your health if you didn't do these things regularly or if you lived in a country where it is hard to get clean water?

12 Make up any board game. Before you start to play, make up five rules so that everyone can play fairly.

Date.................................

Tester.................................

Comments.........................

.............................................

.............................................

# World Traveller

**Note**

To gain this badge you should complete *five* clauses. If you pass five more clauses, you may have another World Traveller Badge.

**Hint**

You will find lots of activities and information in *A World of Ideas*, published by The Guide Association.

1 Make a collection of coins or stamps from at least three different countries.

2 Choose a country with a language other than English.

**Either**
Learn the numbers one to ten.

**or**

Learn how to say the following:

a 'hello'

b 'thank you'

c 'good bye'.

3 Show the tester how to cross a road safely. Work out how to cross the road in a country where cars drive on the other side of the road.

4 Show how you would greet people from three countries in their traditional way, such as rubbing noses (Canadian Inuits), the wai (Thailand) or peace sign (American Indians).

5 Find out what a passport is for and make one for yourself. It must contain a picture or drawing of you, your name, date of birth and address. Draw in entry stamps from different countries.

6 Help to plan and take a trip on a bus, train, boat or plane and draw a picture of your outing. What did you enjoy about it?

7 People in the USA and Africa sometimes cook outside when travelling. Cook something on a camp fire such as marshmallows, sausages or bananas. Make sure there is an

adult with you when you do this.

8 Pack a small bag with the things you would need in order to spend one night away from home. Don't forget a game to play or something to do.

9 Take some photographs while you are on a day trip or holiday. Display and label the pictures, then show them to the tester.

10 Collect some souvenirs from abroad and use them to play a Kim's Game with your Six.

11 Pretend you are sending a postcard to a friend. Make the postcard by drawing a picture of a place on one side of a piece of card. On the back tell your friend about the place.

12 Dress up in clothes to:

a play in snow

b go to the beach.

Know how to protect yourself from the sun and severe cold.

Date ...................................

Tester ...............................

Comments .........................

.............................................

.............................................

# Worldwide

To gain this badge you should:

**Either**

Complete *two* clauses from each of the World Cultures, World Guiding, World Issues and World Traveller Badges.

**or**

If you have already gained the World Cultures, World Guiding, World Issues and World Traveller Badges, you may have the Worldwide Badge.

Date ...................................

Tester ...............................

Comments .........................

.............................................

.............................................

# Writer

**Note**

All written pieces should be sent to the tester in advance. They should be accompanied by a statement from the girl's parent, teacher or Guider confirming that they are her own unaided work.

## Stage 1

1   Write *one* of the following:

- a poem of not more than 20 lines
- a story of your own
- a song (choose a well-known tune) that could be sung by your Unit, for example, at a concert or on Holiday/Camp.

2   **Either**
You have just been carol singing, taken part in a sponsored walk, gone to London for the day, or taken part in a similar event. Write a letter telling a friend all about it.

or

Keep a diary for a month. As well as noting facts, note what you did and where you went. Try to include some of your thoughts and feelings.

3   **Either**
Make up a simple glossary (words and their meanings) of at least 25 words to do with one of your favourite activities (for example, Brownies/Guides, cooking or bird watching).

or

Write a letter inviting someone to your Unit's next Promise Ceremony explaining what the ceremony is all about.

## Stage 2

1   Write *two* of the following:

- a fictional story of 800 to 1,000 words
- a portrait, in about 750 words, of someone close to you, such as a parent, brother, sister or best friend

- a true story (800 to 1,000 words) of something that happened to you when you were young
- an episode for your favourite TV 'soap'
- a collection of poems (at least five) around a theme, for example, the seasons, colours or making friends
- a dramatic sketch, lasting at least ten minutes, for the Unit to perform.

2   **Either**
Write a review (maximum 500 words), suitable for an 'arts' page in the press, of a play, film, exhibition, TV/radio programme or book.

or

Interview someone with an interesting job. Present the interview as a magazine article of a maximum of 600 words.

3   **Either**
Your Unit is putting on a pantomime to raise funds. Draft a letter ▶▶▶

to local firms asking for help with things like props, printing programmes, etc. Explain what your Unit is, what it does and what the money raised will be used for.

or

As part of a twinning scheme, some foreign Guides are coming to stay in your town or village. Write a letter of welcome (maximum 600 words) introducing the area where you live.

## Stage 3

1 Write *two* of the following:

- a poem in a certain form, for example, a sonnet, limerick or haiku
- a radio commercial advertising a Unit event
- a short story (1,000 to 1,500 words)
- the synopsis of a play and its opening scene
- a descriptive account (1,000 to 1,500 words)

of travels either in the United Kingdom or abroad

- a dramatised version of an event in history (performance time 15 to 20 minutes).

2 **Either**
Write a press release giving details about a forthcoming Unit event of interest to the public.

or

Write a 'letter to the editor' about a current issue.

3 Write a letter applying for an imaginary summer job at home or abroad.

4 At the test be prepared to talk about your favourite authors and discuss whether they have influenced your writing style. Bring a review that you have written of one of their books.

5 Bring to the test some standard reference books, for example, a dictionary or thesaurus, and discuss how you use them.

| **Stage 1** |
|---|
| Date.................................. |
| Tester................................ |
| **Stage 2** |
| Date.................................. |
| Tester................................ |
| **Stage 3** |
| Date.................................. |
| Tester................................ |

**Cut me out and colour me in.**

**Bookmark**

# Brownie Magazine

Have you ever seen *Brownie magazine?* Every month it brings you 32 pages full of colour and packed with fun, including:

☆ cool ideas for things to make and do ☆ Go! Challenge fun ☆ features on real Brownies ☆ mind-boggling puzzles ☆ great giveaways ☆ super stories ☆ readers' letters, photos and poems ☆ celebrity interviews ☆ help with badge and Journey work.

**Don't miss out!**

If you would like to find out more about getting your very own copy of *Brownie magazine* posted straight to you, fill in your details below.

Please send me a subscription form for *Brownie magazine.*

Name ............................................................................................................ Age ................

Pack ..........................................................................................................................

Address ....................................................................................................................

Postcode ....................................
BB00

Publications (BB00)
FREEPOST (LON 145)
The Guide Association
LONDON
SW1W 0YA